# The Fake News Dirty Business

Hackers exposed!
Get inside the
lucrative and unethical
world of Fake News

Fernando Uilherme Barbosa de Azevedo

# TABLE OF CONTENTS

ABOUT THE AUTHOR    3
CHAPTER 1 INTRODUCTION    5
CHAPTER 2 INTRODUCTION TO THE SUBJECT    7
CHAPTER 3 HOW DO FAKE NEWS WORK    12
CHAPTER 4 FAMOUS CASES OF FAKE NEWS    20
CHAPTER 5 WHY DO FAKE NEWS THRIVE? 29
CHAPTER 6 FAKE NEWS: WHY DO PEOPLE BELIEVE THEM?    34
CHAPTER 7 HOW FAKE NEWS GO VIRAL    45
CHAPTER 8 HACKERS EXPOSED    50
CHAPTER 9 THE ROLE OF FAKE NEWS IN RECENT ELECTIONS 69
CHAPTER 10 LEGAL ACTION AGAINST FAKE NEWS    72
CHAPTER 11 REPORTING FAKE NEWS ON THE WEB, SOCIAL MEDIA    102
CHAPTER 12 FAKE NEWS COUNTERMEASURES: COUNTRIES 115
CHAPTER 13  DUE DILIGENCE TO SPOT FAKE NEWS    120
CHAPTER 14 FINAL WORDS    126

## ABOUT THE AUTHOR

Fernando Uilherme Barbosa de Azevedo is an electronic, electrical and industrial engineer graduated from Pontifícia Universidade Católica of Rio de Janeiro. He is MBA graduate from Fundação Getúlio Vargas. He has been a programming instructor at Pontifícia Universidade Católica of Rio de Janeiro for 7 years.

He published his first book "Macros for Excel hands on" by publisher Campus/Elsevier at age 27. The book is still sold in Brazil and Portugal.

His first startup business won a prize from the Brazilian Federal Institutional FINEP.

Coming to the United States in 2014, Fernando studied Web Development and Internet Technologies at University of California Santa Cruz - Silicon Valley Extension and also completed the "Innovation and Entrepreneurship Certification" from Stanford University.

Fernando has been featured many times in news media and TV. He was interviewed as a specialist on his field by Forbes, The Entrepreneur, el Nuevo Herald and many other major Brazilian media companies.

Today, Fernando runs 2 internet marketing companies in the United States and has clients in many countries. The companies offer services such as internet marketing, SEO, Online Reputation Managements, pen testing, systems audit, e-commerce, apps and other internet related activities.

He is also a web development instructor for IronHack and weekly speaker at Radio Gazeta.

Fernando considers himself an ethical hacker and thinks that the internet should be a safer place. By advocating against all the unethical activities online that are still present today, he hopes that our leaders and law makers can become aware of these threats and help create laws for a safer world.

This book is dedicated to Fernando's sister Christiane Monnerat.

This book is a series of 5 books related to Internet Technologies and how the internet works. If you like this book, please check out other books from the same author.

# CHAPTER 1 INTRODUCTION

We want to thank you and congratulate you for buying *The Fake News Dirty Business*.

Today, we spend a lot of time on social media. Some rely solely on social media as their means of information. And we generate tons of other information when we read, like, share, comment, and even the time we spend on it.

That massive information generated can be used to manipulate our actions and when it comes to influencing our buying habits, that's my minor concern. News can manipulate our point of view to influence an upcoming election and can we even influence our values and morals.

There are companies specialized in that field. They promote ads, they create viral content, and they use artificial intelligence to best target and influence us.

We will see the origins of Fake News till it become the profitable, unregulated anonymous and dirty business that it is today.

Although people are more aware today about the danger of fake news, companies are also getting better at creating sites that look reputable and also forging sources.

As usual, the purpose of this book is not only to make you aware of hackers can do, but also to advocate for laws that can forbid and punish any manipulative and illegal actions on the internet.

Everyone has freedom of speech on the internet, but it needs to be based on kindness and inclusion. This right cannot be mistaken to hate speech.

This book will demonstrate techniques to spot and report fake news. It is our duty to use it to all fake news, not only to the

# CHAPTER 2 INTRODUCTION TO THE SUBJECT

DEFINITION OF FAKE NEWS

So what, then, is fake news? Before everyone started to use the term more frequently, fake news was what it was: fake. It denotes news or stories that are completely made up, that are false, and that are created to mislead readers. Ultimately, its end involves the manipulation of public opinion.

Fake news has several synonyms: information warfare, cognitive hacking, cyber propaganda, and disinformation campaigns.

Fake news has been extensively used even to report authentic news in scandals cases. From speculations, to deviating opinions, conspiracy theories, news spins, mistakes, and misinformation, fake news has become a representative term for all of it. So let's make a distinction by using a single source: the Merriam-Webster Dictionary.

The Merriam-Webster Dictionary defines the following terms:

Opinion - a view, judgment, or appraisal formed in the mind about a particular matter.

Speculation - an act or instance of speculating.

Misinformation - incorrect or misleading information.

Mistake - to misunderstand the meaning or intention of.

Conspiracy Theory - a theory that explains an event or set of circumstances as the result of a secret plot by usually powerful conspirators.

Spin Control - the act or practice of attempting to manipulate the way an event is interpreted by others.

fake news that harm our interests. You should also spot, report and don't spread fake news that harm other people with different opinions than yours, and even fake news about what you consider competition of your interest.

Thanks again for downloading this book, I hope you enjoy it!

Fernando Uilherme Barbosa de Azevedo

## HISTORY

From its 'discovery' in mid-2016 to its now high-profile status, fake news has managed to denote a lot of things now. Often classified under the realm of misinformation, fake news has managed to gain notoriety when it was used as a political slur. But how was it discovered? And how did it grow to ridiculous proportions?

Before modern times, there only two ways at which the media can communicate: through print and through radio. And both of these media of communication were, at a time, used in the proliferation of fake news. One notable example was that photographs, published in newspapers, were printed depicting those who acted like thorns during Joseph Stalin's reign in the Soviet Union. The radio, which was used by Orson Welles, has at one point, led the public to believe that an extraterrestrial invasion was going to happen.

Another examples of how print was used to spread fake news was the 'Great Moon Hoax' in 1835. The New York Sun ran a series of stories saying that life on the moon has been discovered.

More recently, in 2006, a public television in Belgium reported that the Belgian Dutch has declared independence from the country. At that time, the report was taken to be true.

Fast forward to the new millennium, another type of medium used to spread news was invented: the Internet. Boasting features that go beyond the limitation imposed by space and time, the Internet became the go-to resource for almost all human beings to keep themselves abreast of what's happening around them.

But the arrival of new innovations also means that there are challenges. That's because some people are keen to abuse whatever flaws they can find to either benefit or to harm society.

One of which is the dissemination of fabricated information that dupes the public into thinking that it is true. Fake news than wasn't called as such. In fact, people were hardly aware of the term's existence. Fittingly, it could have been simply labelled as rumors and such.

It wasn't until 2016 that the term 'fake news' finally took hold and achieved worldwide notoriety. And it all started in Europe.

IN THE LAND CALLED MACEDONIA

In Southeast Europe, a tiny speck of a country emerged after declaring its independence from Yugoslavia in 1991. With an estimated population of 1.2 million people in 2017, it placed fourth on the World Bank's 'Best Reformatory States of 2009.'

With a land area of merely 9,928 square miles, it is difficult to believe that Macedonia (not to be confused with the Greek Macedonia) can take the credit as the birthplace of fake news. How did that happen?

In 2016, months prior to the US Presidential Elections, Craig Silverman, BuzzFeed's media editor, noticed a string of fake news stories originating from a town somewhere in Europe. Further investigation unveiled the small town of Veles, the largest city in the region of Vardar.

Silverman and a colleague continued to follow their noses, and before the elections, they have identified at least 140 websites containing made-up news. The interesting thing is, these fake news websites were financially gaining through Facebook.

Yes, early on, the social media giant has facilitated the spread of fake news.

But social media aside, the accidental discovery of these fake news websites has unearthed an unscrupulous offshoot to an already existing business model: paid internet advertising. So who are the culprits?

## THE TEENAGERS FROM VELES

Yes, fake news is the brainchild of several teenage boys. And they did it in the context of the upcoming 2016 US presidential elections. The modus? Plagiarize content from different websites, collate them and skew the information in them, publish them under a new, catchy headline, pay Facebook to target people who hunger for news about Trump, wait for clicks to happen, build website traffic, and earn money from advertisements on destination websites.

At that time when they were still under scrutiny, these boys only had one thing in mind: to earn enough money so they have something to buy clothes and drinks. It's a simple goal conveniently laid out, targeting a nation who was at that time, hyped over news about Trump.

Did they care? The answer was no. In a story published by BBC, a boy from Veles that they have interviewed claimed to have earned as much as 1,500 pounds for his month's work on creating fake news.

Still, he claimed that his friends made more than that. In fact, the teenager they interviewed said that some people in his inner circle were earning a thousand Euros per day.

Because these are kids who actually go to school during the day, and work their fakes news side hustle at night (some of those who are interviewed even claimed to be running their own fake news sites), one would expect that their sense of morality is knocking.

But apparently, that's not the case. In fact, the town mayor made it a point to tell the BBC correspondents that 'there's no dirty money in Veles.'

The mayor even added that he would have been proud that teenagers from his town was able to play a crucial role in potentially skewing the results of a US presidential election.

## SCANDALS ABOUT THE 2016 ELECTION

Cambridge Analytica, a British political consulting firm, has reported influencing the US 2016 elections.

Reports state how Alexander Nix, CEO of Cambridge Analytica, was shown in a secret video broadcast saying they played a major role in the elections. He mentioned performing questionable practices that helped influence voters, and even boasted how he met Donald Trump several times when the latter was still the presidential candidate for the Republican Party.

What exactly did the company do? Apparently, the firm did all the necessary research and analytics. The firm also targeted the voters for Donald Trump's TV and digital campaigns.

Nix had already been suspended and the company mentioned deleting the data after finding out how the data was used and learning it didn't stick to the data protection rules. Facebook also was reprimanded for not informing its users that their user data was utilized in 2014, and in return promises to exert further steps in protecting the people's information.

The US Government also exposed Russian hackers that used ads and social accounts to influence the 2016 elections.

This book will cover more into those recent fake new scandals during this book. For now, we had done a history overview so we can continue to the next chapter.

# CHAPTER 3 HOW DO FAKE NEWS WORK

As it turns out, the teenagers from Veles are not the only ones who are facilitating the spread and use of fake news. The subject now has also gained huge proportions, high profits, skilled PRs, artificial intelligence and big data engineers. There is an elite playing this game - their business is big with highly skilled professionals and their services are offered to big influencers with huge budgets.

FAKE NEWS: A MEANS TO AN END

For fake news to actually make it out there, the creator needs to rely on tools and platforms for publication. These tools and platforms can be legitimate or they can only be found underground. But regardless of a manipulation tool being classified as either legal, illegal, or in a gray area, experience tells us all about how human beings tend to abuse its features, manipulating it for personal gain.

In China, the operation of fake news creators is well-defined. Creators only cater to news items in their own country. With this localized strategy also comes two forms of news content manipulation. First, is the creation of fake news stories, and second, the removal of legitimate content.

For the former, the normal indicators of fake news are present. Different types of content are generated and touched-up as legitimate news and presented for public consumption. The latter involves a more sneaky approach: propagandists bribe website administrators to take legitimate down from wherever it is published. This means that for content beyond the reach of website administrators, methods such as hacking is resorted to.

In Russia, the underground market for fake news is characterized as a one-stop-shop. Underground service providers offer a range of services that covers the creation of fake news stories to its promotion on social media platforms. All of these are done based on the client's demands.

An interesting aspect of Russia's fake news industry, though, is its use of crowdsourcing. The mechanism works in a way that a membership site offers incentives to those who help spread the 'news' out there. The incentives they use are beneficial to their users, with the points re-sellable and usable for self-promotion.

The Russian fake news underground is also no stranger when it comes to voting manipulation. In fact, some underground service providers make it their unique value proposition to say that their systems can bypass security measures in place for digital assets. This includes bypassing captchas, IP addresses, email, registrations, and even social media authentication.

Finally, DIY kits are also offered by the Russian fake news underground to the market. These kits are designed to effectively spam social media platforms and are combined with a botnet for more potency.

In the Middle East, fake news is spreading, but it does have its prohibitions. Mostly, the purpose of creating and spreading fake news is to generate social media followers. However, fake news in circulation must not include pornographic, racist, and illegal content.

In the West, the experience of fake news hits a really personal level. That's because there are tools made available to consumers that allow them to create their own fake new stories. And when users wise up and tap into the underground market for tools they can anonymously use, the perfect recipe of publicizing fake stories is complete.

At the end of this chapter, you will find a list of known companies related to marketplaces for fake news to thrive.

FAKE NEWS: THE METHOD

For the purposes of discussion, note that 'means' indicate what tools are being used to achieve something while 'method' pertains to the manner in which something is done. So how do fake news creator implement their craft? There are five elements involved in the fake news method. The first one involves the title, the second one involves the preview content, the third one involves targeting, the fourth one involves the utilization of tools – legitimate or not, and the fifth one includes the publishing platform. Let's take a look at each of these.

Link Bait title. It is common knowledge that titles ought to grab attention. And in the world of fake news, that largely applies because the potential for content to blow up to unprecedented proportions lies on the eye-catching power of the headline. But what actually amplifies this power is the use of partisan content in the context of political fake news.

Adapting an extremist point of view when writing a fake news headline is important so that it effectively stirs a reaction. It does not matter if the reaction is positive or negative. Once the headline manages to get in to someone's nerves, the job is done.

The preview content. While the preview content is only secondary to the function of the title, it still matters especially in platforms that allows such feature. One platform is Facebook where a post description field is available even in shared links. Another example would be a blog page that has a content preview feature.

What makes the content preview useful is that it provides a gist of a fake news story, thereby decreasing the level of criticality consumers have on a certain headline. In effect, content previews reinforce the tone and the meaning of the headline.

Targeting. Targeting a specific population can take two forms. First, it may involve those who feel strongly for or against a certain topic, person, or place. Second, it may involve a general population in order to cause mass confusion. In the marketing perspective, targeting also includes paying for a content to get more publicity. Again, one common example is Facebook advertising.

Within the social media giant's advertising tools, features such as 'Boost Post' is available as an immediate way to promote certain content. When a content is designed to target a specific audience and money is used to amplify the number of people it can potentially reach, a fake news story can make the rounds faster than the legitimate ones.

Tools. Undeniably, the creation and distribution of fake news stories, although not legal, can be subject to ethical scrutiny in view of its consequences. That's why propagandists often enlist the help of different tools in order to stay anonymous. And as mentioned in the previous section, fake news tool providers have on them a set of services that can be utilized without the client actually doing anything. From a psychological perspective, distancing one's self in the commission of a questionable act is tantamount to saying that 'my hands are clean.'

The publishing platform. It actually does not matter where the fake news ends up being published. But it matters to point out that almost all publishing platforms are not immune to fake news content. For instance, Twitter and Facebook have algorithms in place to detect stories that are considered as spam, inappropriate, or offensive. However, its algorithms can be bypassed by bots. And adding to the injury is the fact that while algorithms to combat unwanted content are in place, another algorithm renders that a story can improve its reach with advertising and consumer behavior. This means that as more people share a story, its reach widens and its engagement level may improve.

It's true: the mechanisms in place to support the proliferation of fake news is becoming organized. This is as long as human beings and technological capabilities continue to find ways to bypass current systems. But in hindsight, anything that the public does not patronize ends up dying a natural death. This doesn't seem to be the case with fake news and that is because motives exist. So what are the motivators of fake news creation?

FAKE NEWS: THE MOTIVATORS

There are four motivators to fake news: character assassination, financial profit, political intents, and personal satisfaction. There could be more out there but based on available literature and the extent at which fake news has developed over emerging utility, we will focus on these four. Let's discuss each of them in detail.

Character assassination. No one is immune to character assassination. Politicians, celebrities, high-profile professionals, and even ordinary individuals. It can also be said that culture influences the proliferation of character assassination. For what purpose? It's merely to smear someone else's reputation in order to destroy one's public image and credibility. And what better way to do that than by spreading fake news (or rumors?) about someone in total anonymity?

Financial profit. Some site owners depend on heavy traffic to earn income with ads. And they end up not limiting themselves to create and spread fake news for their financial benefit. Even if that cost their reputation on the long run.

What seems to be the most scary are the companies behind political campaigns and enterprise reputation wars that make a lot of money to deliver fake news anonymously and make sure they look authentic and highly spread.

Those companies use hackers to copy news sites, or create a fake news site that look very reputable. They craft the fake news to make the most impact on the group they are targeting.

They also make sure an army of bots on social media spread the news creating a viral movement.

But Fake News can even take a huge impact the stock market. In 2013, way before fake news become a household term, the Associated Press's Twitter account was hacked by the Syrian Electronic Army. In it, they tweeted that former President Obama suffered injuries from a bomb going off at the White House. The result? The stock market instantly plunged.

Can this really happen now? We have already experienced the effects of the Great Depression and attempts at hostile takeover in the stock market. We also know of stories about stock market fraud. Now, we can add fake news as one potential instigator to toppling down an economy. How can that happen?

Consider stocks that are both hotly traded and those that are not frequently traded. A company can use fake news in order to manipulate its low share prices and boost its stock value. In reverse, someone with ill intents can circulate fake news about a rather stable company, damage it reputation, and cause its stock value to plummet.

Political intents. Power is, in itself, can cause someone to do a lot of things. In the political arena, this has proven to be a dirty game. Nonetheless, a lot of people devise ways to maintain their stronghold on power. The motivations of politicians in their quest to hold power is a totally different discussion. But using fake news in the name of political advancement is not.

For example, fake news can be used as a front for a smear campaign against a candidate. It can also be used to widen the gap between two or more candidates. More specifically, a fake news creator, in his or desire to tip the odds to favor a certain political person, can spread stories that would cause the public to lose confidence on another political person. This can happen in any presidential elections. Fake news stories placing a candidate in a positive light have proliferated, and the public did not care to verify if those stories were true or not. Regardless, fake news can be used as a vehicle to challenge the current political status quo.

Personal satisfaction. A person need not be psychologically diagnosed with a disorder in order to be compelled to write fake news stories. There are people who are merely thrill-seekers and take to creating fake news to see how far they can go. As they continue to outrun authorities, and as they continue to gain patronage for their craft, their behavior is reinforced. As a consequence, they repeat such behavior again and again.

It should be noted that there are no current legislations involving fake news. No one has even been prosecuted except in the case of slander or libel (there's a more detailed discussion about this in the upcoming chapters). However, there's such a thing as ethical journalism. Fake news is not journalism. It is just what it is: fake.

In the next chapter, let's take a look at some of the famous cases relating to fake news. In the meantime, the list on the next page contains the names in different countries that provide fake news services.

Domains Related to Legitimate, Gray, and Underground Marketplaces and Services

100kfollowers
118t Negative News
BeSoEasy
Boryou Public Opinion Influencing System
Break Your Own News
Breaking News Generator
CoolSouk
Dr.Followers
ftx9
Higym
Indian Facebook Likes
Jet-s
Kwoki
like4u

Quick Follow Now
Shuafans
Siguldin
Slavavtope
SMOFast
SMOService
Social King
TopSoc
VTope
Weberaser
Weibosu
Weibofans
Weixinvips
Xiezuobang
Yunjing Public Opinion Monitoring System
ZiSMO

*Source:*

TrendLabs. (2017). *The Fake News Machine: How Propagandists Abuse the Internet and Manipulate the Public* [Data file]. https://documents.trendmicro.com/assets/white_papers/wp-fake-news-machine-how-propagandists-abuse-the-internet.pdf

# CHAPTER 4 FAMOUS CASES OF FAKE NEWS

Now, for the purposes of demonstrating how simple misinformation can be dubiously amplified, here are some notable cases of fake news.

### PRESIDENT TRUMP DOESN'T WEAR A BATHROBE

What's the deal with bathrobes? In 2017, then Press Secretary Sean Spicer made a bold move to ask The New York Times for an apology following an article is published in February of that same year? The reason? The paper claimed that President Trump watches television in a wardrobe.

Spicer asserted, "I don't think the president owns a bathrobe; he definitely doesn't wear one."

Netizens were quick to react as one by one, photos of the President in his bathrobe graced the World Wide Web and went viral.

### CLINTON – TRUMP ELECTION VOTER FRAUD

The election was over in November 8, 2016 but news about it stayed on thanks to President Trump's active Twitter feed. In late January 2017, YourNewsWire – a certified fake news outlet – published a story that contains this claim:

"A study published by NPR reveals that over 25 million Hillary Clinton votes were completely fraudulent, meaning that the Democratic candidate actually lost the popular vote by a huge margin."

The story gained quite a following and has led to the establishment of the Presidential Advisory Commission on

Election Integrity, whose purpose is to investigate the matter. The committee only lasted for a month and was consequently dissolved but not without concluding that there was no voter fraud.

The truth? NPR didn't conduct the purported study. It was, in fact, a study conducted by Pew Research Center where it reported that, "approximately 24 million voter registrations in the United States are no longer valid or are significantly inaccurate."

However, no lawsuits were filed. Why? NPR went on to say that despite the report findings being taken out of context to be used as a fake news story, there was little evidence to show that it led to voter fraud.

MELANIA TRUMP OR MELANIA TRUMP?

First Lady Melania Trump has an imposter in the White House. What began as a joke soon became a full-blown conspiracy. The conspiracy has it that the First Lady hired a look-alike to fill in for her on some public appearances involving her husband.

Supporters of the conspiracy were also quick to notice a Secret Service agent that looks a lot like her, and a video clip involving Trump who said, "My wife, Melania, who happens to be right here." Snopes.com dismissed this quickly saying that it's fake.

THE ROY MOORE SENATE CAMPAIGN FIASCO

What will you do if you want someone to win a political race? Do a counter-smear campaign. And start with fake news. That's what exactly happened to Roy Moore, a Republican Senate contender from Alabama.

The fiasco started when The Washington Post ran a story alleging that the Moore, then Chief Justice of the Supreme Court of Alabama, has been involved in sexual misconduct involving minors.

Following the bombshell, Moore's supporters came to his defense in what will be an ongoing case after the elections. The supporter's tactics? Discredit the accusers by coming up with fake news information that one of them was arrested for lying; and to circulate a series of tweets claiming that The Washington Post had paid women to come up with stories about sexual misconduct involving Moore. Doug Jones, the Democratic bet, ended up winning the race anyway in an upset victory.

THE POPE ENDORSES DONALD TRUMP FOR PRESIDENT

We're all too familiar with the separation of the church and state. So it was quite a shock when netizens read over a news that Pope Francis actually endorsed then candidate Trump for President.

Speaking with Reuters, the Pope was quoted saying that there were 'difficulties' with Trump and Clinton as presidential candidates and has referred to fake news itself as a 'sickness.'

How did the story gain too much traction, especially on Facebook? Well, it all started when called WTOE 5 News, a website who on its homepage openly declares, 'most articles on wtoe5news.com are satire or pure fantasy,' ran the story. It was then picked up by Ending the Fed, a popular fake news provider.

Following the onslaught, WTOE 5 News decided to seize their operations while Ending the Fed took its story down. However, the latter is still operating as a fake news website.

## DONALD TRUMP'S PLANE RESCUE 200 STRANDED MARINES

This fake news demonstrates how a story, by missing the small but integral details, can totally distort the facts and skew it to benefit (maybe) another party. Such is what happened when in May 2016, Americanmilitarynews.com, published an article about Donald Trump's personal plane flying to Saudi Arabia to rescue stranded Marines after the Operation Desert Storm.

Such story has been corroborated by Sean Hannity, a known political commentator who claimed that the facts of the story has been verified by Trump's team. In fact, the story can still be read on his website, Hannity.com. However, The Washington Post did its own cross-referencing and verification and came up with the real story.

It wasn't Trump's personal jet that picked up the Marines. It was a Boeing 727, part of Trump's fleet under the Trump Shuttle Inc. business. In effect, it was a Trump-branded plane but it wasn't a personal jet. In 1990, the company defaulted on its loans and was eventually sold but not before being contracted by the US Army.

## THE PIZZAGATE CONSPIRACY

Sometimes, it is true that events with a potential to shock the world can start or happen in ordinary places. In 2016, Comet, a pizzeria located along Connecticut Avenue in Washington D.C., hit the spotlight not because of the critical acclaim it received from The Washington Post or the New York Magazine. It was because of the emails shared between presidential contender Hillary Clinton and her campaign chairman, John Podesta.

After Podesta's email account became a victim to a spear-phishing attack, his correspondence to Clinton were hacked and were made public by WikiLeaks. As Reddit and 4chan users consumed the contents of the emails, one theory took form: that references to 'pizza' in the emails actually pertained to Comet and was a code to mean 'child trafficking ring.' However, due investigation has revealed that there was no substantial evidence to support that theory, with the D.C police characterizing the matter as a "fictitious conspiracy theory."

Clinton has been Selling Weapons to ISIS, according to WikiLeaks

In August 4 2016, The Political Insider published a story claiming that Julian Assange, Editor of WikiLeaks, has implied one thing in this interview statement: "Hillary Clinton and her State department were actively arming Islamic jihadists, which includes ISIS." The story claimed that Clinton was selling weapons to ISIS.

Such is not true because what Assange has claimed is that the weapon shipments to Libya in 2011 were approved by Clinton. However, the weapons ended up in the hands of jihadists.

Clinton to Trump: 'He Can't Be Bought and I Would Love to See Him in Office'

Ahead of the campaign period, Clinton has been misquoted by ConservativeState.com and other fake news websites. A self-confessed fake news outlet itself, ConservativeState.com created a derivative quote from what Clinton originally said in an interview with Goldman Sachs. The excerpt, which was published by WikiLeaks referred to Clinton saying that she'd like more successful business people to enter politics.

MEGYN KELLY FIRED AFTER ENDORSING CLINTON, CRITICIZING TRUMP

This is not the first fake news story that got endingthefed.com in trouble. In August 2016, news began circulating about how Kelly was fired by Fox after proclaiming support for Clinton and for criticizing Trump. Megyn Kelly, a former corporate defense attorney, is host of her own show, Megyn Kelly Today. After that episode, the show, was claimed to have experienced a decline in rating and falling behind rival The Rachel Maddow Show in MSNBC.

The fact was Kelly was even offered a $20 million per year contract to remain with the network. But as you would have it, the news, presented in an as-a-matter-of-fact way, has been shared to more than 724,000 people, including the political page that supports Trump: the Colorado for Trump Facebook Page.

## MALIA OBAMA ARRESTED IN CHICAGO FOR DOG FIGHTING, MARIJUANA

This story is proof that even ex-presidential daughters aren't immune to fake news. In May 2017, thelastlineofdefense.online, a self-proclaimed fake news website, published a story alleging that ex-presidential daughter Malia Obama has been arrested with a 'gang of thugs' in Chicago.

The charges? Drugs, drinking, and dogfighting – in a public park.

As if that wasn't enough, the Land of the Free fake news site ran the same story. Only this time, the charge is marijuana use.

Both stories were verified by Snopes.com to be false, proving that the image including Malia Obama in a montage of seven 'gang thugs' was digitally altered to obscure one of the suspect's faces.

## MH370 ABDUCTED BY EXTRATERRESTRIALS

The tales of alien abductions never seem to stop. Whether or not you believe in their existence, there's one story that's proven to be false.

Your News Wire, a website dedicated to false reporting, published a story alleging that a Black Box has surfaced and contains a recording. The message, in military codesign, allegedly says, "Danger SOS it is dire for you to evacuate be cautious they are not human sos danger SOS."

According to snopes.com, this story is not true. That 'eerie message' was purported to be a voicemail to have been received by Ty, a twitter user with the handle @strayeaway. Since the story was published, the handle was altered to make it appear like it is owned by a 15-year old girl.

## DASANI BOTTLED WATER RECALLED DUE TO CLEAR WATER PARASITE

This isn't the first time that commercial products or huge businesses became the subject of fake news. In April 2016, News4KTLA reported that Coca-Cola, the manufacturer of Dasani Bottled Water, has issued a recall of its products in the United States because it found a clear parasite. The story went on to claim that hundreds of people were already rushed to the hospital after reporting symptoms of stomach bloating, rash, vomiting, and fever.

What readers didn't know is that the fake news has used an image of Leptocephalus, an eel larva that is transparent and flat. It is not a parasite.

In response, the Coca-Cola Company issued a statement saying, 'The source of this false and inflammatory information about our brand is a hoax news website. There is no recall of Dasani being conducted in the U.S.'

## RECREATIONAL MARIJUANA NOW LEGAL IN FLORIDA

A timely fake news shared on social media has the title, 'Florida Passes Bill Legalizing Recreational Use of Marijuana.' The source looks like it's an ABC article, quotes Democratic leader Janet Cruz issuing this statement:

"This bill is so much more than legalizing marijuana—it's about legalizing opportunity and prosperity. The state budget was due two weeks ago, and Florida simply can't afford to wait any longer. We deserve a real plan to create new jobs and stimulate our lagging economy, and that's what this bill is."

Well, Janet Cruz is real but the approved legislation is not. The source was later traced to ABCNews-us.com, a fake news website that strives to make it look like it's affiliated to ABC News.

It's important to note that as of this writing, marijuana use is illegal under federal law.

PAMELA ANDERSON DIES AT 50

Even Hollywood stars are not immune to fake news. In March 2018, ABCNews-us.com published a report alleging that the Baywatch star died due to cardiac arrest at Cedar-Sinai Medical Center. The cardiac arrest was reported to have resulted from complications in Hepatitis C and pneumonia.

Despite the news, the actress' social media profile has been active showing that she is alive and well and that the news is a hoax.

Whether or not you're an ordinary individual or you're a person of public interest, the stories above demonstrate that no one is immune from fake news. It is difficult to believe that while there are indications of falsehood from the sources of this news, people are still duped into believing that they are credible sources. Some stories are even picked up by major news agencies or their affiliates and are given a primetime slot.

While the purpose of fake news is sometimes to provide entertainment, it boils upon the people who share to clarify the item they are sharing. A simple note that the story is satire or that it is for fun only can do the trick. You'll see as you progress reading this eBook that there is no stopping fake news outlets from doing what they're doing. It's up to the reader to judge its veracity by taking proper care in validation.

# CHAPTER 5 WHY DO FAKE NEWS THRIVE?

It might just be for the fun of it or something that's more pathological in nature. Whatever the exact reason is, there seems to be no end to the proliferation of fake news. The questions now are: why do people create fake news? Why do people believe in it? Why does it persist even if it's wrong? This chapter is dedicated to answering these questions in the context of the social responses about fake news.

You hoped that when fake news sources were caught spreading lies, they would stop inventing any other stories. You are wrong. In the final chapter of this book you will see a list of sites that take pleasure in writing fictitious stories that are presented as facts. But you should not be so quick on judging them. Some of these sites are self-proclaimed fake news channels. Such a proclamation can be found on their home pages and on their social media sites. But is there a benefit - implicit or explicit - that encourages them to continue to produce fake content? Let's try to answer that in this chapter.

### PEOPLE ARE CONDITIONED TO BELIEVE

Before the Internet, there was television. And before television, there were books. But books, because proper citation is required, are less prone to contain fake information – unless it's the subject of it.

Television, for one, has seen its share of unintentionally featuring fake news. One recent example is when ABC Reporter Brian Ross claimed that President Trump ordered Michael Flynn to establish contact with the Russians.

Despite Ross clarifying such report, and ABC News issuing an apology, the damage has been done.

Not every one of those who watched the initial reporting were able to watch or read the clarification or the full apology.

The implication? Those people would have shared such information to people they know on their network. They might have taken to social media and commented about it.

Some may have written a blog about it. The possibilities for sharing what's initially incorrect is endless. That's because a story can be shared in different ways

And speaking of stories being shared in different ways, there's always a chance that the initial facts can be distorted until the original version is significantly altered.

The result? A totally fabricated story. If you're familiar with the game called 'Pass the Message,' you know what this means.

So the adage that goes, 'if it's on the internet, then it must be true' hardly fits the system of truthfulness we ought to be following today.

On one hand, such perceived authority is partial as media outlets now are improving their standards of vetting their stories. On the other hand, we can't also claim that something is false because it is being shared. This brings us to another concept.

In social media, the more Likes, Shares, Retweets, +1's, Pins – you name it – the more authoritative a story appears.

It's the same philosophy that consumers also fall victim to: if a restaurant has many diners, the food must be really good.

So social media metrics are now also being used on the user-level to create an impression as to the truthfulness or credibility of a story.

## FAKE NEWS VALIDATES PEOPLE'S CONFIRMATION BIASES

It's not exactly good but we all have our own sets of biases. One of which is called the confirmation bias, and it is defined as the tendency for us to look, to interpret, to favor, or to recall information in a way that reinforces our pre-existing beliefs.

To illustrate, if we've always believed that someone is a better President, we'll be prone to look for information to sustain that belief, consume content that aligns with that belief, share information relating to that belief, and interpret information that reinforces that belief.

Now, take note that this is a type of bias so it does not align with the context of objectivity. As a result, even if we don't do our own due diligence, we're bound to share something merely because it fits right into our belief system.

One thing that can be gleaned from this is that the confirmation bias clouds our own ability to be critical. This effectively removes our tendency to ask ourselves about whether or not what we're reading is true.

PEOPLE WANT TO BE A PART OF THE CONVERSATION

How would you like to be 'in?' How would you like to be among the people to take advantage or to be a part of a hype? You probably say that you'd like to be a part of something trendy. But if the question is clearer, you might think twice. If someone asks you, 'Would you like to be a part of a party that never happened and post on social media a party photo?', what would you answer?

The idea is the same when it comes to creating fake news. People want to be a part of the conversation that's why they tend to like it, comment on it, and even share it so they can show it off their social network. The idea that they're a part of something matters so much that it merits a shareable quality.

One example would be in times of natural disasters. You're not a stranger to photos being shared about the devastating effects of hurricanes and earthquakes. The intention to inform what's going on is there but what if the image or the video used is something taken years ago in a different place? If you know that such is the case, would you still share it?

Images or videos used in an out-of-time and out-of-place contexts qualify as fake news. In the same manner, comments can become a part of fake news if made on a story that never took place at all or has already taken place but is presented as a part of a recent event.

For example, if a hurricane is in progress on one state and someone shares a photo of a previous hurricane from another state then comments, 'At the moment,' would you be sympathetic if you know that such is not the case on the sharers current location and that the photo was taken at a different time and place?

People need to express sympathy in times of calamities. It's human nature. And they share whatever they see because it's their sense of sympathy that takes over. To actually make it a point that an image or a photo is old may attract backlash. So those who know don't say anything, and those who don't say a lot of things.

## PEOPLE DO IT ON PURPOSE

It is undeniable that some people are well-versed when it comes to spreading lies. Unfortunately, some people's tendencies or impulses are significant enough to warrant a valid psychological diagnosis.

As opposed to pathological liars though, ordinary people whose way of life involves spreading rumors are rampant. They find thrill in spreading lies and find satisfaction seeing the reactions of affected people. Yet some just spread lies for the sheer fun of it. These people have a name: trolls. Trolls are people who deliberately, secretly, and cleverly piss people off through the use of dialogue. That dialogue, sometimes, involves false stories.

But for most, the act of sharing fake news is something not deliberate. They don't even have an idea that what they're sharing is false. All they know is that they're sharing information. In effect, the burden of proof lies on the person who has an inkling that such a story isn't true.

SOME TRUTHS ARE THAT BIZARRE

Yes, there are stories that are too good to be true, but are indeed true. For example, sometime in September 2017, a forest fire was raging in Portland, Oregon. The viral photo that was shared was taken in high-resolution and was posted on Facebook. In the photo, the background shows the raging blaze while golfers in the background were putting about.

Surprisingly, some people expressed doubt on the reality of the image. Some claimed the photo was edited. But the photo is real.

What happened in this case points to the nature of the reality we're living in: if it generates awe, it must be a lie. If it doesn't, it must be true. One can argue, then, that our being accustomed to the strange realities of life leads us to take comfort in fiction.

Now, if fakes news is fake, why would people believe them? Let's answer that question in the next chapter.

# CHAPTER 6 FAKE NEWS: WHY DO PEOPLE BELIEVE THEM?

If the news are fake, why people believe them?

## COGNITIVE BIASES: A SOURCE OF UNREASONABLE BELIEFS

In the psychological perspective, cognitive biases are a collection of irrational judgment patterns that deviate from the norm. Since content consumption is most often attributed to a person's inclinations, biases come into play for the purposes of subjective satisfaction, justification, and interpretation. Here are some of the applicable cognitive biases that support the contention that belief in fake news is has something to do with a person's psychological predispositions.

Ambiguity effect. This is the tendency for people to formulate their conclusions based on options with known probability over ones that don't. In the context of fake news, ambiguity effect draws upon a belief system that may also be influenced by other cognitive biases.

To illustrate, a reader of fake news about a philandering politician may be inclined to believe the accusation as true if there are no known rebuttals to such claim. Besides that, the fake news is presenting the news in a truthful manner. What makes matters worse is when the reader has prior belief that that politician is philandering even if it's not proven.

Anchoring. Also called focalism, this is the tendency to anchor or to rely on one piece of information when making decisions. Commonly, the anchor is the first information acquired by the person about the subject.

For example, if a person initially reads about a celebrity being a snub to his fans, the person will hold that information and the next time he reads something about the same celebrity, he is more inclined to believe it as true because of an already existing piece of information.

Attentional bias. This happens when a person's judgment is affected by his recurring thoughts. For example, if a person has always thought of a country to be a land of terrorists even without hard evidence, he is more likely to believe a story that talks about the same thing. That's regardless of the news being fake or not.

Availability heuristic. This happens when a person draws conclusions based on how quickly examples or similar information come to mind (availability). In the case of fake news, a person tends to believe them because he might have thought about a recent and similar information. Otherwise, he would exude some criticality over the news if he cannot think of any similar cases that points to the news as a fact.

Availability cascade. This involves the prevailing knowledge of the masses and presupposes that if the same information is repeatedly used in public by the public, it must be true despite the presence of an indication that it is not. For example, the Pizzagate scandal wouldn't have blown out of proportion if it weren't circulated by people over social media. This led to media coverage which further intensified interest in the story. In the end, many have believed the conspiracy theory because of repetitive encounters.

Bandwagon effect. Also called herd behavior or groupthink, this is the tendency to believe a piece of information because the public indicated that it is true. In more specific cases, if a person closely follows a specific group of people who share the same principles, anything the group says is believed by the person to be true. This is what happened at the turn of the millennium. The Y2K phenomenon has caused unreasonable behaviors among a selected group of people because they believed that the world was really coming to an end.

Conservatism. This is the tendency for a person to stubbornly hold on to what he believes even if it's proven to not be true. In the case of fake news, a person would have believed in it first and defends such belief even if the people he knows have presented him with new evidence that proves the contrary. As a result, the unreasonable belief is maintained and may even be shared to unsuspecting people.

The continued influence effect, another form of cognitive bias, is similar to conservatism in a way that a person refuses to believe corrected information.

Courtesy bias. When a person fears that he will offend someone by giving an unpopular opinion, he'll give something that is socially acceptable and disregards what is true. So if a person is surrounded by people who firmly believe in a fake news story, he is more inclined to provide an opinion that falls within his peers' belief system rather than risk starting an argument.

Hyperbolic discounting. This is the tendency for people to believe more strongly a single person who is at risk than a group of people who are at risk. For example, if a fake news story claims that Hillary Clinton has been misaligning government funds to her personal account, a person subject to hyperbolic discounting may believe that story to be true than when the story claims that all Democrats in government positions have been doing the same thing.

This type of cognitive bias is somehow influenced by a person's pre-existing sentiments about another. Meaning, if the reader dislikes Hillary but likes some democratic political figures, he will have a greater tendency to believe the news singling out Hillary.

Illusion of validity. This is the belief that one's opinions are valid because it is supported by information that is consistent with that belief. Sometimes, this happens when an unsuspecting person is exposed to fake news that tell of the same story. For example, when the news that Malia Obama was arrested in Chicago, two fake news outlets were discovered to have made discrepant claims over the charge. However, both claimed that Malia was indeed arrested. Reading that, a person will be inclined to believe that Malia was arrested although the charge is not definitive.

Mere exposure effect. This is the tendency to like or to dislike something because of sheer familiarity with it. In the context of fake news, this is the tendency to believe in something because one has had prior exposure to it. This brings into light the quality of such exposure. But since this is a bias, it can happen that a person's belief may have been influenced by previous information about a subject or a person, true or not.

As an example, a fake news saying that Paris Hilton has another adult video taken and leaked online might be taken as true because similar thing happened to her in the past that happened to be true.

Negativity bias. This is the tendency of a person's belief to take form about an unpleasant news because they recall equally unpleasant memories in the context of the news. For example, a person might have visited another country as a tourist and has some locals steal his belongings. Because of that, when he reads a fake news attempting to tarnish that country's reputation, he will be inclined to believe it to be true.

Ostrich effect. This happens when a person ignores a negative situation. This implies that a person who believes in fake news knows that it is fake and yet continues to believe that it is true.

Rhyme as reason effect. An example of this bias would be, 'If it's on the Internet, it must be legit.' Thus, if an argument has a rhyme, a person would believe it to be true.

Selective perception. When the news that the Pope endorsed Donald Trump's candidacy, pro-126 individuals spread the information faster than a wildfire. That's because getting endorsement from a Pope is a huge blessing over one's integrity to lead, Trump supporters were ecstatic. But none of the people within this group has ever pointed out that the story was fabricated – which it was.

In summary, the cognitive biases presented above share common characteristics. First, there is a desire to validate one's beliefs. Second, that such belief will be defended even if it's built on the grounds of untruths. And third, because such belief fits well in the system of a person, he or she is more prone to share it.

Now, let's consider the social perspectives of why people believe in fake news.

NEED: A CHALLENGING SOCIAL DRIVER OF BEHAVIOR

Let us start by considering this: not one person actively desires for false information. No one rejoices over misinformation, either. And no one appreciates being lied to. But since the fake news phenomenon infiltrated people's social lives, it seems that those statements have become debatable. That's because people nowadays consume fake news at an unprecedented rate. And they not only consume them; they share them. What ever happened to 'do not spread false information?' That question highlights our discussion in this section as we reveal the social perspective as to why people believe in fake news.

THE NEED FOR CERTAINTY

According to Hunt Allcott and Matthew Gentzkow from the National Bureau of Economic Research, Americans have been exposed to an estimated average of 14 fake news stories during the 2016 elections. And that's not strange at all. That's because there's been an unspoken social unrest among the American people that started in prior administrations.

In hindsight, Hillary Clinton is widely known in the political arena, but some controversies surrounding her actions and decisions during her political tenure have come under scrutiny. So enter Donald Trump. When pitted with someone who has become a part of the country's political history, the newcomer was recognized as the trigger to restart American politics.

It is no surprise, then, that when Allcott and Gentzkow published the results of their research, it revealed that more people were inclined to believe news stories that favored Trump than those of Clinton. What about those news stories? Well, they're fake news stories.

This phenomenon illustrates the society's need for certainty. The talk about change has been present among all political aspirants in history. But it was that phrase, 'Make America great again,' made by a political that might have appealed to the masses. No one in the history of the United States has spoken so sharply but simply other than Donald Trump.

That brings us to the concept of simplicity as the main component of certainty. If people communicated with simplicity, if they make their assertions in a direct way, they exude an air of certainty. That's regardless of them speaking based on hard evidence or merely from their own assumptions.

It has been a norm for politicians to observe propriety in their rhetoric. They can't be too harsh, they can't be too judgmental, and they can't be absolute. That's because critics are watching and are listening. As a result, they tend to sugarcoat their statements.

But at a time when society is hungry for change, and at a time when there's express economic, political, and social turmoil, people seek refuge on the one that can speak their thoughts the exact way they want it. Trump was doing it.

As a consequence, even if news about Trump were exaggerated, manipulated, and fabricated, the public took comfort in them. It effectively removed the public's sense of due diligence. They were getting what they wanted to hear. They were satisfied.

## THE NEED FOR SPECIFIC OUTCOMES

Related to the need for certainty is the need for specific outcomes. If a claim is made with a tone of certainty, the justification should outrightly show what can be done about it.

In The Philippines, incumbent President Rodrigo Duterte delivers his promises with conviction and he uses non-conventional language to do so. With a mouth full of profanities, he was many times quoted to say that he will kill everyone who are involved in the country's drug trade.

While a third-party observer might have criticized that kind of language from a potential President (he is still foul-mouthed as a President) – which some people actually did – his statement alluded to a definite course of action – killing. And with cessation of life, it can be concluded that the war against drugs will end.

Politicians are known to make promises. And in countries like The Philippines, the people have had enough of hearing about ideal platforms which end up not being realized anyway.

The constant exposure to politicians who beautifully present their promises and who end up not delivering any has been a mainstay. With Duterte's arrival in the political scene, the people developed a perception that finally, every Filipino's yearnings to have a better life may be realized after all.

Is President Duterte immune from fake news? The answer is no. Just like President Trump, President Duterte has called out the proliferation of fake news about him. And just like Trump did to CNN, the New York Times, and other media outlets, Duterte has also called out local media outlet, Rappler as a 'fake news outlet.'

For both needs, a person has to have this quality in order to believe things like fake news: the belief expressed in the fake news story should be in line with his belief system.

# A NOTE ABOUT THE ACCESSIBILITY OF INFORMATION AND PRIOR KNOWLEDGE

To say that everyone actually believes fake news is to generalize. There are indicators that not everyone gets carried away by fake news despite it being motivationally gratifying. And that happens for three reasons.

Knowledge of the truth. When a person knows what is true, he tends to dismiss all fabricated claims. But to put this in context against the popularity of fake news, how many people actually come forward and speak of the truth as matter-of-factly? There will always be rebuttals from the other side. And when a person is fighting alone against a battalion of unreasonable believers, his chances to prove his point effectively diminishes.

Lack of knowledge. For some people, the lack of knowledge causes them to believe even something that is fabricated. The phrases, 'You don't know what you don't know' and 'what you don't know won't hurt you' applies in this situation. When confronted with things or ideas that they are not knowledgeable about, people do one thing: they turn to those who know about it. They ask questions and they do their own research.

Now, doing one's research is a risky step nowadays. That is because fake news outlets have become clever by presenting fake news stories in an authoritative manner and by using credible-looking websites. ABC News wouldn't have known that they have a website called ABCnews.com.co had the latter not been exposed for its fake news contents. It is easy to persuade people at times only because they're not armed with the caliber of knowledge needed in order to combat fabricated information. At times, they are simply not informed.

Accessibility of knowledge. For some people, getting access to truthful information is hard enough. What complicates the situation is that fake news outlets are so good at promoting their content out there that their information is easily accessible in the public domain. The result? People will be exposed to fabricated information. And at times when they can't do their down diligence, they turn to grapevine as their source. And if their grapevine source is a person they trust, they tend to give up due diligence altogether.

Now, in the final section of this chapter, let's take a look at the political reasons why people believe in fake news.

## THE POLITICAL PERSPECTIVE OF FAKE NEWS

Public trust in the media have been declining. In a report published by marketing communications firm Edelman in 2018, it is revealed that only 42% of Americans trust the media.

For both media and government institutions, the report shows that the United States has suffered a 37% decline in trust ratings the highest among the countries of its group. The country joins Italy, Brazil, South Africa, India, and Colombia as the group that suffered 'extreme trust losses.'

On the opposite end, the countries with 'extreme trust gains' are China, UAE, South Korea, Sweden, Malaysia, and Poland.

In America, the brands CNN, New York Times, TIME, Washington Post, ABC, and Newsweek used to be synonymous with 'trust.' That has not been the case since recently. And the addition of fake news in the mix only served to reinforce such declining reputation.

In 2017, David Ignatius, a Washington Post Opinion Writer, cited a Pew Research Center poll showing that 72% of Americans believe that news organizations tend to favor one side when covering social or political issues. The findings may be considered valid. But the question is: is it enough to justify the high consumption rate of fake news?

The answer to that question is 'no.' You can't justify patronage of fake news just because you don't trust legitimate news outlets. But in a society characterized by 'taking comfort where they find it,' that's hardly the case. People may be comfortable looking for news stories even if it's not real. If it's not meant to entertain them, it's just about reading something perceived as partisan content for the sake of it. All in all, it boils down to the existing belief systems that people have built for themselves that needed to be satisfied.

In the next chapter, we'll look at how fake news spreads like a wildfire.

## LACK OF KNOWLEDGE

News have started to cover the phenomenon of fake news, but the subject was still unknown for a lot of people. Although we expect people to become aware of the fact that there are fake news being spread on the internet, we also expect fake news increasing in quality. So we can find better imitations of reliable websites, better content and even links that prove what's being faked.

Always make sure the news come from a reputable source. You can even check if other major reputable media sites are also covering the same subject.

If you ever run into fake news, make sure you report it. We will talk about reporting fake on websites and social media.

Be aware that commenting, disliking and even share it to point out it is fake news may cause it to increase virality. If you ever feel like interacting with fake news even to quickly report to others that it is fake news, make sure you report it as well.

# CHAPTER 7 HOW FAKE NEWS GO VIRAL

This chapter is a consolidation of the means and the methods being employed by fake news creators in order to maximize the dissemination potential of a fake story. The bulk of the discussion centers on the Fake News Triangle created by Trend Micro, a security firm based in California. It also includes facts and figures taken from its report, The Fake News Machine: How Propagandists Abuse the Internet and Manipulate the Public, which was published in 2017, as well as information sourced from reliable websites online.

THE FAKE NEWS TRIANGLE

The Fake News Triangle illustrates how three components work together in order to spread fake news. The three components are: motivation, dissemination services, and social media. Let's take a look at them one by one.

MOTIVATION

In sum, the motivation for creating fake news is to influence readers to think in the same way as the fake news creator. In order to do that, the publisher needs to put together content that is characterized as misleading, biased, fabricated, and, in most cases, non-existent.

In Chapter 2, we mentioned that there are three primary motivators for creating fake news. These are character assassination, financial profit, and political intent. Now, it has to be made clear that the intention of the fake news creator need not be negative. It can also be positive, such as creation of fake news in order to boost a person's image. The bottom line, regardless of the motivation, is to influence people to adapt a linear kind of thinking as the content leads them to that end.

DISSEMINATION SERVICES

This component includes the tools, the services, and the platforms used in order to create the fake news content. In Chapter 2, we have seen a list of known providers of fake news services, which is a combination of underground and gray-area service providers. What we did not cover in that chapter are the costs associated with enlisting such services.

Nothing comes for free, especially those transactions involving unethical practices. In line with that, the absence of solid ground to criminally sanction fake news creators, service providers, and dissemination platforms are limited to non-existent. So if you are to avail of the services of fake news provider, how much money do you need?

A report by published by MIT Technology Review highlights that for $55,000, you can bring down a journalist, and for $200,000 you can incite a street protest. These figures are true as evidenced by actual cases.

THE CASE OF ALBERTO ESCORCIA

In Mexico, there's such a term as a 'troll gang.' Troll gangs are a group of anonymous people who are being paid by the hour in order to create thousands of tweets and retweet them several times with the intention of discrediting journalists, attacking them and their work, and to make fake stories go viral.

Alberto Escorcia is one of these journalists. In an interview he had with Tanya O'Carroll, Adviser on Technology and Human Rights for Amnesty International, Alberto said that it all began on the second anniversary of the 43 students who have disappeared in Mexico in September 2014. At that time, a street protest was organized. As a response troll gangs began their attack against journalists, activists, and organization who supported the protest's goal.

Alberto said that he downloaded all tweets by using the hashtags the trolls were tweeting on, sorted out the accounts, and reported them to Twitter. And while the accounts ended up being blocked, new ones have been created. In a matter of two days since the troll gangs warned journalists to not join the street protest, 10 of them, including human rights groups, public figures, and Alberto himself, received death threats.

But Alberto only became aware of the existence of these troll gangs when in 2012, he became an active member of #YoSoy1342. #YoSoy1342 is a student movement that aimed to stage a street protest in the wake of Mexico's presidential elections. Using a pseudonym, Alberto started to call on some of the protests. In doing so, that's when he became aware of something behind Twitter's tweets and retweets trail. He says,

"At first their tactics were unsophisticated. They were basically spambots that would flood Twitter with thousands of automated tweets. They were a nuisance, hijacking hashtags we were using to organize protests and filling them with spam and false information."

Now, spambots are an easy kill for Twitter. In a matter of seconds, spam tweets were identified and were promptly blocked. But what happened next attests to the motivation factor in the Fake News Triangle: spambots were replaced by troll gangs. This was when things got a little complicated for Alberto. And had it not been for the person who approached him out of guilt in 2014, he would not have been able to figure out what's going on.

The repentant troll confided to him that she was being paid almost $2,500 per hour in order to run 150 accounts and publish tweets with the intention of undermining the #YaMeCanse protests.

Other journalists and vocal critics of what's happening in Mexico are going through the same experience as Alberto. At present, Alberto is still under the government's 'protection measures' by the National Mechanism for the Protection of Journalists.

In sum, the troll gang's modus operandi is to maintain a drip of negative articles in a four-week period. Each article is to be retweeted 50,000 times and coupled with a direct attack through commenting on the journalist's articles. The estimated costs of doing all of these? $55,000, according to Trend Micro.

## THE CASE OF THE RACIAL SLUR AT ST. OLAF COLLEGE

In May 2017, David Anderson, the President of St. Olaf College in Minnesota addressed its student body in an email saying, "We've confirmed that the note was not a genuine threat."

The threat is in reference to a note left on a black student's car the month before saying (not the complete note),

"I am so glad you are leaving soon. One less [N-word] this school has to deal with. You have spoken up too much. You will change nothing. Shut up or I will shut you up."

Another student took a photo of the note and posted it on Twitter. From there, things began to spiral out of control. Classes were suspended, classes were boycotted, and a sit-in protest has been organized.

Following the investigation, it was discovered that the note was a hoax and the author has been reprimanded. In the end, the investigation was closed because the target chose not to file a criminal report.

If this situation was driven by the spread of fake news, Trend Micro says that the estimated cost would be $200,000.

At the end of this chapter, you'll find a list associated with the costs in enlisting fake news services.

## SOCIAL MEDIA

Nowadays, the easiest way to reach hundreds and thousands of people is through social media. While this is not the publication platform that fake news creators utilize per se, it is the ideal distribution platform. That is because the financial aspect of creating fake news is embedded in the advertising model of social media platforms. That is, a fake news story is published on a website; that post will be shared on social media; the post will be promoted in order to increase its reach and engagement; visitors will click on the link; and they will be redirected to the fake news website. In turn, advertisers will pour money into the website to take advantage of the traffic.

Now, social media is not the only enabler for fake news to spread. Note that wherever you can paste a link for everyone to see, you can spread fake news. This includes forums or membership sites, blog post comment sections, and messaging apps.

In the next chapter, let's focus on the costs associated with enlisting the services of what Trend Micro calls, 'Public Manipulation Campaign Service Providers.'

# CHAPTER 8 HACKERS EXPOSED

A team of writers and campaign architects can prepare the perfect content and forge the perfect evidences in order to make people believe in the fake news they want to spread.

However, it takes a good team of hackers to make sure the technical side of things look real enough.

Hackers have access to software that can copy a website within minutes to replicate perfect copies of websites that already have established good reputation. By having the green lock by the site's URL address and catching a website domain name that can confuse people, they can pretend to be a reputable source.

For example; a hacker trying to pass as CNN could register a domain cnnlatestnews.com or even try something as cnn.latestnews.com

Also, they can easily create websites with Newspapers like templates that seem very professional and reputable.

When a hacker uses cryptocurrency to pay for the internet access and VPN (Virtual Private Networks), they become completely anonymous on the internet.

Virtual Private Network is a series of internet addresses that users can use protecting their real internet addresses (IP). A lot of companies that provides VPN services, state that they do not keep any logs of their user being impossible to track which user was using an IP in a given time.

If those companies would keep a log with those access, the FBI could link an IP to an user that was posting fake news for example.

However, hackers can buy their internet services with cryptocurrency and pre-paid cards or even have several lawyers of IPs, making it impossible to be discovered.

MORE SOFTWARES

Hackers also have access to software that can help spread their news. They can spam millions of emails, they can create fake social media accounts that do shares, comments, likes. They create millions of articles linking to the fake news in order to boost it's search engine ranking.

Although social media giants and search engine giants try to minimize the use of software to create user accounts and simulate social signals, hackers can still do it using services to break captcha and also use disposable emails and phone numbers.

Crowdsource platforms also can be used. They pay cents for their users to share, like and comment and it's quite easy to start a campaign like this.

Captcha was a technique created to verify that it is human indeed trying to use a website in the other side of the screen. Captchas can ask letters and numbers, images, math problems and clicks to verify the humanity of the users. However there are paid services that collect the solution of these questions and are easy to integrate with software.

The smarter big sites get, the smarter hackers get as well.


BIG DATA AND ARTIFICIAL INTELLIGENCE

In 2018, Facebook faced a privacy crisis that started with a company called Cambridge Analytica. It's known that this company works with many politicians trying to influence their votes to their favor.

Using Facebook apps like quizzes, tests and games, companies like this can gather massive information from social media users. Adding techniques of big data and even machine learning (or Artificial Intelligence), their software can promote content to users in order to influence them.

It's also important to point that companies that want to influence our buying behavior, votes or even culture, are getting the most of the new technologies to help them influence and persuade.

Machine learning can not only help these companies to write fake news in ways to target a category of individuals, but also tell when to post it and feed back on the results to improve their tests.

PENETRATION TESTS

Hackers have access to software that scan websites and servers in search of any vulnerability. Some of these offer even offer the option to attack or give out important information that the hackers can use to find a way in.

For servers and websites of media sites, that can be extremely dangerous for fake news and removal of legit news. Hackers can gain access to edit, delete and add articles once they gain access.

SOCIAL ENGINEERING

When it comes to manipulate you in a world where you are anonymous, there is no limit to it.

Hackers often use social media and search engine to gather information from their victims. They also have other tools to discover as much of information of the victim like emails, phone numbers, address, friends and family.

Once they have that information, they craft a personalized email of friend request that has more chances of being accepted. Sometimes, even an online friendship happens before the hackers deliver their attack.

With a link or a file to download, they can gain control over someone's machine and whatever is typed on that machine even usernames and passwords for other sites.

Getting access to confidential information on a business or politician or even a news media site, they can add, edit and delete news.

For fake news agencies, having a team of expert hackers can be extremely useful not only to create fake news but also to bury or delete legit negative news for the entity they work for.

The most dangerous news it that, hackers and dubious internet marketing services are not hard to find on the deep web and they are available for spot jobs.

Plus they can be contacted and paid for in full anonymity.

Using VPS or a Tor Browser for example, users can search for the "hidden wiki" where they can find links to a lot of services that are illegal or at least should be considered illegal.

By using encrypted text messages with apps such as Telegram, Signal or Wickr, they can send messages privately. Also, by using temporary emails and encrypted emails services such as ProtonMail, they can also maintain anonymity.

Payments made with pre paid credit card and cryptocurrencies such as Bitcoin are also used to protect their names.

As you can notice, there are a lot bad practices that should be regulated on the internet in order to keep fake news and other illegal activities away.

HACKED SOCIAL ACCOUNTS

Social Media platforms are constantly working on methods to increase its security to prevent any kind of hacking and spreading of fake news. Countries like Venezuela, Bahrain, and Myanmar are deeply affected with almost similar cases. The method is that hackers hijack verified accounts. Verified accounts are accounts that are known to be as public interest, meaning they have lots of followers. Knowing that their content get lots of likes, comments and shares, their accounts are being hacked and cloned to spread fake news under their name.

Hackers can use social engineering to send a spoofed email to the account owner asking to click on a malicious link, download a virus or even enter their credentials on a cloned website. By doing that they are able to get credentials to their social and email account.

This hack method is called "Double Switch" wherein they first take over a verified accounts, and change its layout and profile. After changing its name and handle, the identity of the whole account has changed. That is described as the first switch.

The second switch, on the other hand, is when the hackers creates a new account on the name of previous account hacked, with the same handle since it will be available then.

This is done to bewilder followers. Most activists from Venezuela and Bahrain are victimized. The accounts are manipulated to spread fake news.

This "Double Switch" hacking method seems to attack countries with political unrest. The aim is to urge more divisiveness and chaos.

FAKE NEWS AND ERRATA

Although is not fully associated with hackers, unscrupulous newspapers and journalists are also reported to be using this technique.

The technique is used to create a fake news with parts of documents, interviews and photos. The article is spread out on social media and featured on their website.

After publishing the fake news, they also make an article with an erratum fixing the misinterpretations of the first article, however the erratum is not posted on social media and not featured. It's often hidden and used only for legal purposes. Hackers can help a newspaper hide a link of an erratum to most users and also help the first fake news article to be more visible in social media and search engines.

MICROTARGETING

Microtargeting is the technique to segment people into different categories in order to create content specific for each group in order to influence them.

Microtargeting can also take into consideration events on the group's life to influence them. For example, if a city has a snow storm forecast, ads with content about the storm can be displayed to residents of the city. Examples can even be more specific to you, marketers can target people whose birthday are near, sending content about birthday ideas or fake researches about what other people with the same age are doing. Even the type of writing, and the type of link bait titles can be different to target specific niches.

Marketers like these can have hundred of fake articles and they can use ads to target each group of individual using a compelling and related history to influence them.

Not only social media, but a lot of sites can also gather information about their visitors with forms, web browser cookies and visitors clicks and views. They can use it for themselves or sell for third party microtargeting ads campaigns.

Different sources of databases can be merged together with big data and machine learning to improve the results of their campaigns.

Microtargeting is so effective and so influential that is even considered a dubious technique for legitimate marketing companies. In the hands of hackers and unscrupulous marketing professionals, the technique can be extremely dangerous.

PUBLIC MANIPULATION

Before moving on, let us be clear on three things. First, while some of the service providers listed below operate in the black market, some of their services can be used for legitimate purposes. Second, these companies have tailored their services with respect to their target audience and the prevailing digital culture in their respective countries. This means that some of the terms and conditions for services offered in China, for example, may not be applicable in the US market. Third, to fully understand why instigators would want to engage the services of a business operating in the black market, one should consider accountability. Instigators who opt for black market services with the intention to create fake news stories are protected by anonymity.

Compiled from different sources, these are the prevailing costs one has to pay in order to spread fake news. . It should be noted that it is possible that these sources also have derived information from other sources, so it's not to be used as a definite guide. No, it does not specify the names of the providers or any information pointing to their websites. Use it for educational purposes only. Figures are in US Dollars based in 2018.

**GENERAL**

Create a celebrity with 300,000 followers in a month: $2,600

Discrediting a journalist: $55,000

Instigate a street protest: $200,000

Manipulate decisive course of action: $400,000

Capture 100,000 signatures on Change.org: $6,000

10,000 petition signatures or votes: $1,065

25,000 petition signatures or votes: $2664

Content eraser: start from $50

## CONTENT CREATION

500 to 800-word article of a propaganda disguised as journalistic work: $15

1,000 to 1,500-word article of a propaganda disguised as journalistic work: $30

## CONTENT DISTRIBUTION ON PAPER AND ON TELEVISION

On national news: $116

On provincial news: $72

On IT news: $174

On finance or business: $131

On healthcare: $189

On real estate: $131

On Baidu news feed: $116

Press release distribution: $802

Classified ads of an un-reputable paper: $266

Unclassified article publication: $21,641

Commercial news sites: $5,328 - $9,768

## CONTENT DISTRIBUTION ON SOCIAL MEDIA

On YouTube main page for two minutes: $621

20 trending videos on YouTube for two minutes: $7,992

VIP social media services: $106 - $124

100 dislikes on a YouTube video: $1.7

100 comments on a YouTube video: $2.6

1,000 group joins: $11

First 1,000 – 1,000,000 views on YouTube: $3 - $999

500 followers on Instagram: $25

500 retweets on Twitter: $2 - $130

Auto-likes on Facebook: $25 as a monthly subscription

2,200 auto-likes on Facebook: $150 per month

10,000 auto-likes on Facebook: $800

Eight comments per day: $45

1,000 comments per month: $250

1,000,000 YouTube views package with 50,000 likes: $3,150

## Analytics

10 keywords: $1,850

20 keywords: $4,175

10,000 site visitors: $17

**Social Media Promotion**

WeChat celebrity post: $69,500

Weibo famous user post: $180,000

100 subscribers, friends, likes, video views on Instagram: starts at $0.23 - $0.4

100 follows, likes, and retweets on Twitter: starts at $0.34

100 YouTube subscribers: starts at $0.66

100 YouTube likes, video views, and full video views: starts at $1.55, $0.3, or $0.23

1,000 video views: $0.89 - $4.26

10 comments: $2.84

1,000 channel subscribers: $50

Trend a video: $222 - $266

1,000 page likes: $17 - $31

1,000 Instagram subscribers: $3 - $15

**Vote Manipulation and Click Farms**

One server with 30 phones: $4,925

One server with 50 phones: $7,815

One server with 100 phones: $14,524

## Instagram Packages

100 followers, 100 likes: $3

500 followers, 500 likes: $6

1000 followers, 1000 likes: $10

2500 followers, 2500 likes: $25

5000 followers, 5000 likes: $40

15,000 followers, 15,000 likes: $100

## Twitter Packages

100 followers, 100 retweets, 100 favorites: $4

500 followers, 500 retweets, 500 favorites: $10

1000 followers, 1000 retweets, 1000 favorites: $12

2500 followers, 2500 retweets, 2500 favorites: $25

5000 followers, 5000 retweets, 5000 favorites: $40

10,000 followers, 10,000 retweets, 10,000 favorites: $100

## YouTube Packages

1000 views, 100 likes: $20

5000 views, 500 likes: $72

10,000 views, 2500 likes: $180

50,000 views, 10,000 likes: $585

100,000 views, 10,000 likes: $685

1,000,000 views, 50,000 likes: $3150

## Facebook Packages

500 likes: $10

1000 likes: $17

5000 likes: $40

10,000 likes: $70

20,000 likes: $130

40,000 likes: $230

## SoundCloud Plays

500 plays: $4

2500 plays: $12

10,000 plays: $30

50,000 plays: $90

100,000 plays: $170

1,000,000 plays: $999

## Twitter Packages

5,000 followers: $29

10,000 followers: $39

20,000 followers: $68

50,000 followers: $146

100,000 followers: $275

THE PUBLIC OPINION CYCLE

Using Lockheed Martin's traditional cyber kill chain, Trend Micro has come up with the Public Opinion Cycle in order to illustrate how instigators – the people behind public manipulation campaigns – achieve their goals when it comes to changing the public's opinion to match their own. The cycle involves seven phases. Let's discuss them one by one.

RECONNAISANCE

This steps has three goals: to define objectives, to establish who the audience is, and to understand the audience.

In its explanation, Trend Micro has utilized the Sufficiently General Control Theory framework which categorizes the 'means of ruling' as applied to general groups. The ruling categorization ranges from least immediate but most effective to most immediate but least effective.

Audience worldview information. The instigator seeks to understand how his or her target audience perceive the events around them.

Audience historical view information. The instigator seeks to understand how his or her target audience perceive events in historical terms.

Descriptive information. The instigator seeks to consider the facts about certain events.

Economic influence. The instigator seeks to influence his or her target in an economical way.

Long-term threats. The instigator seeks to influence his or her target by considering the latter's well-being and health, including those of the latter's descendants.

Immediate threats. The instigator seeks to influence his or her target by issuing threats.

The categories above are arranged according to the sets of actions or processes that are most effective but are time-consuming to the least effective but are not time-consuming. So a closer analysis reveals that the third category is where an instigator can maximize his goals for manipulation despite it being in the middle in terms of effectiveness. This is because the most effective tactics take too much time and that the least effective tactics are difficult to cover up.

## WEAPONIZATION

Now that the instigator is armed with the knowledge about his or her target audience, his or her next step would be to build an array of weapons. One of those weapons is fake news. It can in this discussion that fake news is only of the many weapons that an instigator can arm himself or herself with because in consideration of pushing a certain form of content to become popular, he or she only need to inject volumes of it in publishing platforms.

## DELIVERY

This is the moment when the instigator takes his or her campaign to the public. Now, the instigator will not readily deliver his manipulation campaign to its intended audience only because they have been identified and understood. What the instigator does is to create a leeway at which he or she can naturally insert the campaign. An instigator can achieve this by destabilizing his or her target audience's current belief systems so that they can be receptive to changing it. In other words, the instigator has to cause his or her target to question their existing cognitive constructs so that a gap of what they currently believe and what they ought to believe (which will be influenced by the instigator) can be created. The gap is where the manipulation campaign will center; it will become the means to achieve an end.

And how is delivery achieved? We discussed earlier in this chapter that there are tools available in the gray areas and underground areas of the marketplace. At times, an instigator may opt to go DIY provided that he or she has the tools to put a manipulative campaign into motion.

## EXPLOITATION

To exploit a manipulative campaign, the instigator has to be familiar with how the target audience formulate and express their opinions. As such, the concept of peer pressure, the bandwagon effect, and the fear of social alienation comes into play.

Peer pressure is achieved when a person, who thinks differently from his peers, finds out that he is among the company of people who think otherwise. As the target individual, his constant exposure to people who share a common belief that happens to be different from his will causes his resistances to erode little by little. Depending on his resolve to defend and to stick to what he believes, a person will either separate from the group or will eventually realign his beliefs with his peers.

The power of a manipulation campaign to persuade individuals or groups lies on the quality of the pressuring group. If they are people of authority and if they are people who are respected by the target individual, there's a greater chance of persuasion.

As more and more people who exhibit the result of the manipulation campaign come about, and with the sustained power of the campaign itself, there will come a time when they become a dominant faction. This leads to the bandwagon effect. When this point has been reached, it will be easier to manipulate other people who are a part of the minority.

The final 'phase' in the exploitation of a manipulative campaign involves taking care of the 'breadcrumbs.' Often, people who find themselves in the minority position prefer to simply keep their silenced over matters that they feel strongly about. This especially happens when they are in the company of a group of people who exhibit an equally strong belief which is in contrast to that individual.

But a person who chooses to keep his or her silence may not be eventually persuaded. Does this mean that the manipulative campaign is working? The answer is yes. That is because the beliefs of the minority end up being suppressed. A person's choice to keep his or her silence is not necessarily a sign of dissent or consent. It is just a sign that when he or she speaks up, he or she will get alienated by the majority.

PERSISTENCE

The objective of this phase is to increase the visibility of a manipulative story by maximizing its reach. Now, this reach is not simply anyone. It is a pre-defined audience that support the new belief. The mechanism? It involves promoting the story on various platforms and inserting a call to action – direct or indirect – for supporters to share the story and to increase its circulation. This explains why some stories on social media go viral while some, despite perceived popularity and appeal to the masses, only barely reach that level. From a psychological standpoint, this is called 'the snowball effect.'

SUSTAINMENT

Trend Micro explains this phase by referring to the Overton Window. Also known as the 'window of discourse,' it captures the range of ideas that are tolerated in public discourse. The framework is that ideas which were initially perceived as outrageous may eventually end up being accepted by a certain group of society. So in this context, what is the key to facilitate such change in belief? It is sustaining the manipulation campaign.

The Overton Window has six stages which operate in a cycle, namely:

Unthinkable

Radical

Acceptable

Sensible

Popular

Policy

To cite an example, in the 4th century, the prevailing belief centered on the geocentric model that that the Earth was the center of the Universe. From the Earth, the sun, the moon, the stars, and other planets revolve. It was a widely accepted at the time because of the absence of knowledge. It was not until Nicolaus Copernicus developed the heliocentric model in the 16th century that this belief has been challenged became widely accepted.

In reference to the Overton Window, one would have expected that with Copernicus, when going public with his model, has been met with great alienation and criticism. After all, his model is a challenge to the very own astronomical knowledge at that time. But it actually did not happen that way. What Copernicus actually did was to simply publish his manuscript. At the time of the publication, other astronomers already have an idea about his work. Then, Johann Albrecht Widmannstetter, Pope Clement VII's secretary started to give lectures presenting Copernicus' theory. One of the audiences were the Pope himself and several cardinals.

Three years later, Nikolaus von Schönberg, then Archbishop of Capua, wrote to Copernicus encouraging him to publish him to publish the full version of his model. Among the skeptics?

Martin Luther and his collaborator Philip Melanchthon. Both believed in what The Bible says about the Earth being a stationary entity and the sun being the moving entity.

So despite not having published a definitive statement of his model until his death, Copernicus had already completed it. The embodiment of which is called De Revolutionibus. He dedicated his work to Pope John Paul III who succeeded Pope Clement VII after his death, and had Andreas Osiander write an unsigned preface. Osiander was a German Lutheran and a theologian.

It is widely believe that this preface was key to minimizing the brewing public debate at that time and influenced Copernicus' work from being tagged as heretic. There were news that the work should be banned but it never actually happened.

Although very much in contrast to the goals of manipulation being discussed in this chapter, Copernicus had done something that rendered his work easier to accept.

First, he capitalized on the public's receptiveness at that time by allowing other astronomers to be aware of his work. Second, he targeted an audience which was the prevailing authority in terms of what the people should believe: the church. Third, he dedicated his work the Pope. And fourth, he turned to another respected person of the church to actually introduce his published work. So when it comes to sustaining the goals of a manipulative campaign, it pays to consider authority, relevance, urgency, and receptiveness. For once an audience's opinion is eroded in some way, it is easier for someone to cause a bigger erosion in the long run.


ACTIONS ON OBJECT

So what comes next after an instigator achieves his or her goal? The options are on the table. If an instigator is following a commercial campaign, the next step would be to sell a product. But in this context, we are talking about something political. So in extreme cases, street protests would be the next phase. Boycotting a political rally is another. Effectively showing other forms of lack of support for a candidate is yet another thing. In the end, the goals of the instigator is what will eventually dictate how far a manipulative campaign should go once it achieves its goal to change an audience's opinion.

## REINFORCEMENT

There is no such thing as a cooling period when it comes to manipulative campaigns. That is because other manipulators lie in wait to take advantage of an unstable condition. That being said, the instigator should make it a point to go back to this target audience to cement their changed belief system. It is all about making sure that the changed belief is sustained, if not made permanent.

How is this done? Instigators can opt to continue manufacturing content that reinforces the existing beliefs and push them out for public consumption. Once this phase is done, the cycle repeats itself.

In the next chapter, let us take a look at the role of fake news in recent elections.

# CHAPTER 9 THE ROLE OF FAKE NEWS IN RECENT ELECTIONS

2016 US PRESIDENTIAL ELECTION

Russian hackers interfered with the 2016 presidential elections with a massive cyber-attack against state voting systems. The Russian hackers were reported to be leaking e-mails that destroyed Hillary Clinton's campaign. Aside from leaking e-mails, the hackers also disseminated fake news through social media sites, specifically Facebook and Twitter. More than 80 accounts were created and bots were spread out through the internet.

An e-mail sent to the chairman of Clinton's presidential campaign, John Podesta, alerted him about a 'compromise' in the system. The alert ordered him to change his password immediately. However, this alert turns out to be a phishing e-mail which successfully gained access to over 60,000 e-mails in Podesta's private account. On October 2016, Julian Assange of WikiLeaks announced that they were in possession of Podesta's e-mails and has released 2,000 of all the leaked documents. Clinton's party did not confirm nor deny the legitimacy of the stolen documents. The leaked documents, however, hugely affected Clinton's candidacy.

At least one half of the news posted on Twitter were said to be fake and that they came from bots. Facebook was heavily criticized for its incompetence and incapability to stop fake news from spreading in its own platform. However, Facebook discovered hundreds of fake accounts connected to a Russian troll farm which bought $100,000 in advertisements that targeted the audience of the US presidential election. The ads were mainly about critical social issues aimed to divide the nation with different views and opinions. Facebook reported that more than 100 million Americans have seen the posts ran Russian-based operatives and hackers.

The CIA, FBI, and National Security Agency are confident with the involvement and interference of the Russian government in the 2016 US presidential elections. The aims of the interference were to damage campaigns and to inflict instability in the US.

## GERMANY'S FEDERAL ELECTION

The Bundestag hacking occurred in May 2015, with the intruders stole documents that were 16 gigabytes worth. The hackers checked through hard drives and duplicated documents that were fresh and recently created. To make sure they leave no trace, they had software reinstalled.

A total of 14 computers were hacked, and one of them is German chancellor Angela Merkel's computer. Her computer was mainly manipulated by the hackers, sending e-mails to the members of Christian Democratic Union (CDU) under her name. Just like what happened to Podesta, the e-mails sent are phishing mails that contain a link. The link, when clicked, infects the computers involved with a virus.

German IT specialists found a trace of code linked to Russian hackers which were also linked with the attack on the US Democratic Party.

Once again, it was rumored to be Russian hackers and the government interfering with yet another election, attempting to launch another misinformation campaign.

The German government, particularly anti-cybercrime agencies, took precautionary measures by launching "fact check" sites.

This is to prevent any kind of fake news from spreading. One of the goals of the German agencies is to initiate a fake news hunt.

## CAMBRIDGE ANALYTICA SCANDAL

As previously stated, Cambridge Analytica, a political consulting firm funded by Rebekah and Robert Mercer, was reported to work with several famous politician campaigns.

The technique used was developed at Cambridge University's Psychometrics Center, although the center declined to work with Cambridge Analytica, a researcher from the institution named Aleksandr Kogan decided to join the company.

Aleksandr Kogan created some sort of quiz as a Facebook app – "thisismydigitallife". Everyone who took the quiz got their information taken by the program. However, a loophole inside the Facebook API allowed the profiles of the friends of takers to be accessed, taking more information. More than 200,000 users took the quiz, unaware that they had their friends' information taken as well. Facebook exposed raw data from more than 80 million profiles to Kogan.

THE BIG FIVE MODEL OR OCEAN SCALE

The Big Five Model is a instrument for personality traits to describe personality.

The 5 factors are openness to experience, conscientiousness, extraversion, agreeableness, and neuroticism. Getting the first letter of each factors, we have the acronym OCEAN.

Combined with micro targeting and the data captured with Aleksandr Kogan's quiz, Cambridge Analytica had the tools to create articles and ads to influence a voter with a specific message.

This history shows the dangers of people's data on the internet that can have a huge manipulation impact when combined with microtargeting ads and fake news. Hackers can explore those techniques to enhance their success rate.

# CHAPTER 10 LEGAL ACTION AGAINST FAKE NEWS

Before we start the legal procedures, there are some important steps that people can take when dealing with fake news.

Although all processes against fake are not usually as fast as a company or celebrity needs, there are some actions that can be taken right away to try to smooth the impact of fake news. The user that is suffering from Fake News can quickly report on their social media account that is suffering from Fake News and ask their supporters to report the posts to the social media network. Plus, the account owner can show that has taken the matter into their own hands to handle the problem and to represent their values. They can also issue pros releases stating the true story.

When replying to fake news and offenses online, remember the gold rule of social media: "be positive or be quiet". Disable accounts from all members that may have trouble controlling their temper. And remember: getting print screens of fake news is extremely important when filing a suit.

Let's start the subject on the legal side.

Is it even possible to take action against fake news? The answer is it's possible but it's not probable. Why? This chapter focuses on the legal concepts related to fake news by referencing a law that all Americans are all too familiar with: The First Amendment and the offshoot legal rules that go with it.


BACKGROUND: THE FIRST AMENDMENT

According to Cornell Law School's Legal Information Institute, a platform dedicated to open access to laws in the United States, the First Amendment protects the freedom of Americans in three areas.

First, Freedom of Religion. This clause prohibits the government from preferring one religion over others and from passing any legislation that establishes an 'official religion.' This clause also reinforces the separation of the church and the state, where the latter must present substantial argument if it does decide to interfere to the affairs of the church.

Second, Freedom of the Press or Freedom of Speech. This clause give rights to individuals to express themselves without sanction from the government. In matters of content regulation in free speech, this clause requires that the government must have a compelling reason to do so.

Under this clause, a private individual is not held civilly or criminally liable for any statements he or she makes against another person or a topic as long as his or her claims are based on truth or on honest opinion.

Third, Freedom to Petition or to Assemble. The right to establish one's belief and to consequently associate one's self to such beliefs is implicit in this clause. It states that an individual has the right to join an assembly or a petition lawful and peaceful purposes. Such a right is also implicit in the two other Amendments: the Fifth and the Fourteenth Amendments.

From the three clauses above, it is clear that the Freedom of the Press or Freedom of Speech includes fake news. However, to interpret this jurisdiction, you must also be aware of two specific stipulations in this clause.

First, that the government may interfere with speech that incites violence or disturb peace. And second, that government interference on the spread of fake news may be interpreted as censorship. These stipulations provides the answer as to why, all these years, people and websites who spread fake news are not prosecuted in court on each count of misinformation. Now, this brings into question: what if you're a victim of fake news spread with a malicious intent to harm your reputation?

# DEFAMATION LAWSUIT: A VICTIM'S MAIN LEGAL RECOURSE

A defamation lawsuit seems to be the most viable option for a civilian or a business entity who falls victim to fake news. At the civilian level, the lawsuit that an individual files against another is called tort. In this case, the case is called a tort of defamation. But what constitutes a defamation lawsuit?

A defamation lawsuit can take two forms: slander for oral statements and libel for written statements. In order for the plaintiff to win a defamation case, he or she must be able to demonstrate or prove four things:

That the statement is false but is presented to be the truth

The republication rule: that the false statement must have been passed on in writing or through oral communication

That the fault amounts to negligence at the very least

That damage or harm befalls the person who is the subject of such statement

Now, the burden of proof or showing of fault lies on the prosecutors of a civil case. In essence, the prosecution has to be able to prove that the false statement is actionable. This means that the defendant could be held liable for the defaming statement regardless of his or her state of mind. In other words, the defendant, despite not knowing if such information is false, could have taken care to verify its truthfulness before spreading it.

On a business or a public-personality level, defamation lawsuits can only succeed if the prosecution can prove that such statements were made with malicious intent. In other words, that the defendant made such statements with or without care whether or not they're true. But in contrast to a civil case, businesses or public personalities who claim defamation must be able to demonstrate actual malice in a convincing and clear manner as opposed to the burden of proof in the former.

## BREAKDOWN: PROVING OR DISPROVING DEFAMATION

All defamation claims must be defended with the truth. As such, the 'truth' becomes the central argument on both the prosecution and defense parties. With truth considered to be an 'absolute defense' on all claims of defamation, either parties must be able to:

Show that the statement is false, and

Establish and demonstrate the fault(s) of the defendant

Now, in defamation cases, there are two types of privileges you need to be aware of: absolute privilege and qualified privilege. Both privileges lies on the defense, but their utilization in court varies from state to state. To define:

Absolute privilege are statements made in a certain context or venues. For example, witness testimonies in a defamation case are all considered to be absolute privileges. That's because such statements are subject to sanctions if proven untrue, as they're made under oath.

Qualified privilege can be used as an effective protection by the defense provided that:

That the alleged defamatory statement was made in good faith,

That the alleged defamatory statement was made by a person who is interested in its context or is obligated by a sense of duty to do so,

That the alleged defamatory statement was made to people who consequently had interest or duty on the matter, and

That the alleged defamatory statement was made without malice.

To simplify, qualified privilege takes place if the defendant has made a false statement because of a moral, social, or legal duty to do so to someone who has a corresponding interest in receiving it.

This communication must be free of malice and must not be taken advantage of in order to spread misinformation that will damage a person's reputation.

In effect, the defendant must be able to prove to the court that the false statement was made without an intention to malign the affected individual and that he or she has taken the steps necessary to verify the accuracy of such statement before believing it to be true.

A simple example of someone using qualified privilege in court would be a defense party who calls employers to provide character reference to a previous employee involved in a defamation case.

## FAKE NEWS LAWSUIT: DISTRIBUTION OF ACCOUNTABILITY

Once an individual files a defamation lawsuit over fake news, who's going to be accountable? Generally, it's everyone involved in the republication of such information.

Now, this republication rule states that the information has to be passed from one person to another in order to be qualified as such. In effect, if a plaintiff can track all people involved in spreading such misinformation, he or she is free to sue all of them.

## THE CHALLENGES IN A DEFAMATION LAWSUIT

While filing a lawsuit is the easy part, the process of court proceedings is the challenging part. Apart from the burden of proof and utilization of privileges, the plaintiff can face the following factors that may contribute to a defamation case moving forward:

Monetary Damages. Whether or not fake news spreads faster than truthful news is not the question. That's because once a fake news is out, there's not telling the breadth of reach it has on time and on space. Once it's out, it's out. So the question for the victims is: is monetary damage really what they're after? A reputation that's already tarnished may be partially recoverable. But will money as a retribution fix everything?

Legal Costs. Related to monetary damages, plaintiffs also face the challenge of legal costs. It is estimated that lawyers involved in defamation cases charge somewhere from $400 to $500 per hour. What if the trial drags on for months? Will the monetary damage be able to recover the costs? What of the plaintiff's additional exposure to the media if the case gets covered? What of the emotional impact the trial has on top of the psychological and moral effects of the false statement?

Post-Trial Ramifications. If monetary damage is paid and legal costs covered, what would be life like for the parties involved? In a society where free speech is protected by law, it is inevitable that two sides to the argument will ultimately surface. One that condemns and one that supports the defendant. As a result, those who condemn the defendant are inclined to support the plaintiff and vice versa. What would life be like for both parties once the trial is over?

## THE NATURE OF DEFAMATION LAWS

What is the truth? Why is the concept incorporated in the First Amendment? The basic stipulation is that the truth will eventually win. The First Amendment was built on that premise. And such premise was useful. Then.

In the kind of society we're living in now, that hardly applies. That's because arguments over the veracity of a certain information is often marred by personal opinions and unverified points for argument.

To demonstrate the truth, we need to arm ourselves with every bit of verified information that are proven to be true. The challenge is, we only have a brief time for almost everything. And in case where a person is really serious about proving that a certain statement is a lie, tons of hours may be required. If done outside the court of law, the monetary equivalent of those hours may not be recoverable.

In hindsight, there are instances where falsity actually wins. That's because the opposing parties have simply given up. But in the exercise of presenting arguments of falsehood or truthfulness, the parties involved have demonstrated how freedom of speech actually works in real life.

Freedom of speech is not figurative. In this context, it is the act of proving or disproving itself that sees freedom of speech in action. In conclusion, truth may not always win but without freedom of speech, it may not have a chance of eventually winning.

HOW TO SPOT FAKE NEWS

Perceived credibility. This is the main tool that fake news sources use in order present themselves with a speck of truthfulness. This begs the question: how do you spot if news is true or not?

Check the website or the print source. What's the prevailing reputation of the source? Recognize the some digital and physical publications publish contents that are classified as parodies. This is one important detail that most people are oblivious of. In a time-poor society, it's something that's relegated to a secondary step in fact-checking.

A parody means is an imitation or an exaggeration of something to create a comic effect. In some cases, a parody is presented as a satire.

For this reason, parodies written or spoken in a satirical way should not be taken as the truth in face value. Readers or recipients of such information now are tasked to verify whether what they're presented with is true or not.

Yes, the burden of proof should lie on the source of the information. However, a smart receiver should also be able to take steps to verify a statement's truthfulness before sharing it further.

Check the story. This is related to fact-checking. A website, snopes.com, is a fast-checking website that's been helping a lot of people ascertain if an information is true or not.

Another fact-checking website you need to be aware of is FactCheck.org. This is a website dedicated to proving whether or not political information is true.

Cross-reference the news with one of the websites presented at the end of this chapter. These are websites known to publish fake news content and have been identified by PolitiFact.com as a part of its collaboration with social network giant, Facebook. This list was last updated by PolitiFact in November 2017.

Do your own research. Be a sensible source of republished information. Do your own homework by following related links, doing your own research, and so on.

The best way to become a credible source of information is reference verified sources. It's also one of the best ways to stop the spread of fake news.

GUIDE TO FAKE NEWS WEBSITE

Note that this list was last updated by PolitiFact.org in November 2017. Please visit their website for a more updated list.

| WEBSITE | TYPE OF SITE | LOCATION |
|---|---|---|
| 16WMPO.com | Imposter site | Scottsdale, AZ |
| 24online.news | Imposter site | Panama, Pa. |
| 24wpn.com | Fake news | Veles, Macedonia |
| 24x365live.com | Fake news | Kobenhavn, Denmark |
| 247NewsMedia.com | Fake news | Kumanovo, Macedonia |
| a-news24.com | Fake news | Dhaka, Bangladesh |
| ABCNews.com.co | Imposter site | Phoenix, AZ |
| actualidadpanamericana.com | Parody site | Scottsdale, AZ |
| AlabamaObserver.com | Imposter site | Toronto, Canada |
| AmericanFlavor.news | Fake news | Panama, Pa. |
| AmericanNews.com | Fake news | Burlington, Mass. |
| AmericanPeopleNetwork.com | Fake news | Veles, Macedonia |
| AmericanPoliticNews.co | Fake news | Came up as available for use |

| | | |
|---|---|---|
| AmericanPresident.co | Fake news | Tblisi, Georgia |
| AmericanToday.us | fake news | Los Angeles, Calif. |
| AMPosts.com | Fake news | Chesterbrook, Pa. |
| ANews24.org/ | Fake news | Panama, Pa. |
| AngryPatriotMovement.com | Fake news | Scottsdale, Ariz. |
| Anonjekloy.tk | Fake news | Amsterdam, Netherlands |
| AntiNews.com | Fake news | Amsterdam, Netherlands |
| ArmyUSANews.com | Fake news | Panama, Pa. |
| AsAmericanAsApplePie.org | Parody site | Scottsdale, Ariz. |
| AssociatedMediaCoverage.com | Parody site | Scottsdale, Ariz. |
| Attitude.co.uk | Some fake stories | London, UK |
| Aurora-News.us | Imposter site | Santiago, Chile |
| AwarenessAct.com | Some fake stories | Panama, Pa. |
| BabylonBee.com | Parody site | Berkley, CA |
| BB4SP.com | Fake news | Midwest City, Okla. |
| BeforeItsNews.com | Fake news | Scottsdale, Ariz. |

| | | |
|---|---|---|
| BenjaminFulford.typepad.com | Fake news | Shen Zhen Shi, China |
| BestThings.us | Some fake stories | Davao, Philippines |
| BlackInsuranceNews.com | Some fake stories | Ridgefield Park, N.J. |
| Blog.VeteranTV.net | Parody site | Panama, Pa. |
| BlueLineStrong.net | Some fake stories | Panama, Pa. |
| BlueVision.news | Fake news | Panama, Pa. |
| BlueVisionPost.com | Fake news | Panama, Pa. |
| BostonLeader.com | Parody site | Toronto, Canada |
| BreakingNews247.net | Imposter site | Paris, France |
| BreakingNews365.net | Imposter site | Paris, France |
| BreakingNewsBlast.com | Fake news | Orem, Utah |
| BreakingTop.world | Fake news | Panama, Pa. |
| BostonTribune.com | Parody site | Scottsdale, Ariz. |
| BuzzFeedUSA.com | Fake news | Scottsdale, Ariz. |
| CannaSOS.com | Some fake stories | Scottsdale, Ariz. |

| | | |
|---|---|---|
| Channel18News.com | Imposter site | Scottsdale, Ariz. |
| Channel24news.com | Imposter site | GoDaddy |
| ChristianTimesNewspaper.com | Imposter site | Scottsdale, Ariz. |
| ChristianToday.info | Fake news | Scottsdale, Ariz. |
| CivicTribune.com | Fake news | Scottsdale, Ariz. |
| CivicTribune.com | Imposter site | Scottsdale, Ariz. |
| City-Herald.com | Some fake stories | Wild West Domains |
| ClashDaily.com | Fake news | Scottsdale, Ariz. |
| CNewsGo.com | Fake news | Scottsdale, Ariz. |
| CNN-Business-News.ga | Imposter site | domain available |
| CNNews3.com | Imposter site | Scottsdale, Ariz. |
| CoffeeBreakForYou.com | Fake news | Brea, CA |
| Conservative7.com | Some fake stories | Panama, Pa. |
| Conservative101.com | Fake news | GoDaddy |
| ConservativeArmy88.com | Fake news | Scottsdale, AZ |

| | | |
|---|---|---|
| ConservativeDailyPost.com | Fake news | Panama, Pa. |
| ConservativeFlashNews.com | Fake news | Panama, Pa. |
| ConservativeInfoCorner.com | Fake news | Came up as available for use |
| ConservativePaper.com | Fake news | Panama, Pa. |
| ConservativePoliticus.com | Some fake stories | Brea, CA |
| ConservativeSpirit.com | Fake news | Chesterbrook, Pa. |
| ConservativeView.info | Fake news | Panama, Pa. |
| DailyBuzzLive.com | Fake news | GoDaddy |
| DailyFeed.news | Fake news | Panama, Pa. |
| DailyInfoBox.com | Fake news | Panama, Pa. |
| DailyNews10.com | Imposter site | Scottsdale, Ariz. |
| DailyNews5.com | Imposter site | Scottsdale, Ariz. |
| DailyNewsPosts.info | Fake news | Chesterbrook, Pa |
| DailySidNews.com | Fake news | Veles, Macedonia |
| DailySnark.com | Parody site | Scottsdale, Ariz. |
| DailyStormer.com | Some fake stories | Worthington, OH |

| | | |
|---|---|---|
| DailySurge.com | Fake news | Alexandria, Va. |
| DailyThings.world | Fake news | Panama, Pa. |
| DailyUSAUpdate.com | Fake news | Scottsdale, Ariz. |
| DamnLeaks.com | Fake news | Colorado Springs, Colo. |
| DefenseUsa.club | Fake news | Panama, Pa. |
| DemocraticMoms.com | Fake news | Panama, Pa. |
| DemocraticUnderground.com | Fake news | Kensington, Md. |
| DenverInquirer.com | Imposter site | Toronto, Canada |
| DepartedMe.com | Fake news | Chesterbrook, Pa |
| DepartedMedia.com | Fake news | Chesterbrook, Pa. |
| Disclose.tv | Fake news | Passau, Germany |
| DIYHours.net | Fake news | Panama, Pa. |
| DonaldTrumpPOTUS45.com | Fake news | Free Union, Va. |
| Duffelblog.com | Parody site | Nassau, Bahamas |
| EmpireHerald.com | Imposter site | Scottsdale, Ariz. |
| EmpireNews.net | Parody site | Chesterbrook, Pa |
| EmpireSports.co | Parody site | Sellersburg, IN |
| En-Volve.com | Fake news | Chesterbrook, Pa. |

| | | |
|---|---|---|
| ENHLive.com | Fake news | Brea, California |
| FactRider.com | Some fake stories | GoDaddy |
| FederalistTribune.com | Fake news | Brea, California |
| FedsAlert.com | Fake news | Scottsdale, Ariz. |
| FirstPost.com | Some fake stories | Mumbai, India |
| FlashNewsCorner.com | Fake news | Panama, Pa. |
| FloridaSunPost.com | Parody site | Toronto, Canada |
| FocusNews.info | Fake news | Scottsdale, Ariz. |
| ForFreedomWorld.com | Fake news | Kobenhavn, Denmark |
| Fox-News24.com | Imposter site | Scottsdale, Ariz. |
| FreedomDaily.com | Fake news | Scottsdale, Ariz. |
| FreedomCrossroads.us | Parody site | North Waterboro, Me. |
| FreedomsFinalStand.com | Fake news | Scottsdale, Ariz. |
| FreedomJunkshun.com | Parody site | GoDaddy |
| FreeInfoMedia.com | Fake news | Panama, Pa. |

| | | |
|---|---|---|
| FreeRepublic.com | Some fake stories | Fresno, CA |
| FreeWoodPost.com | Parody site | Scottsdale, Ariz. |
| FreshDailyReport.com | Fake news | Veles, Macedonia |
| GiveMeLiberty01.com | Fake news | Scottsdale, Ariz. |
| GlobalPoliticsNow.com | Fake news | Kumanovo, Macedonia |
| GlobalRevolutionNetwork.com | Fake news | Kumanovo, Macedonia |
| Guerilla.news | Fake news | Gradsko, Macedonia |
| GummyPost.com | Fake news | Scottsdale, Ariz. |
| HalfwayPost.com | Parody site | Beaverton, Oregon |
| HealthyCareAndBeauty.com | Some fake stories | Berlin, Germany |
| HealthyWorldHouse.com | Fake news | Kumanovo, Macedonia |
| HeightPost.com | Some fake stories | Athmuqam, Pakistan |
| HigherPerspectives.com | Some fake stories | Scottsdale, Ariz. |
| HoustonChronicle-TV.com | Imposter site | Scottsdale, Ariz. |
| Huzlers.com | Parody site | Panama, Pa. |

| | | |
|---|---|---|
| IdeaSpots.com | Some fake stories | GoDaddy |
| ILoveNativeAmericans.us | Some fake stories | Kosovo, Serbia |
| IndiaTimes.com | some fake stories | Gurgaon, India |
| IndependentMinute.com | Some fake stories | Toronto, Canada |
| InterestingDailyNews.com | Fake news | Orem, Utah |
| IsThatLegit.com | Fake news | Toronto, Canada |
| JewsNews.co.il | Some fake stories | Shiloh, Israel |
| KBC14.com | Imposter site | Scottsdale, Ariz. |
| KCST7.com | Imposter site | GoDaddy |
| KF13.com | Imposter site | Brooklyn, NY |
| KMT11.com | Imposter site | Scottsdale, Ariz. |
| Konkonsagh.biz | Fake news | Ashanti, Ghana |
| KRB7.com | Imposter site | GoDaddy |
| KTY24news.com | Imposter site | GoDaddy |
| KY12News.com | Imposter site | Scottsdale, Ariz. |

| | | |
|---|---|---|
| LadyLibertysNews.com | Fake news | Kirkland, Wash. |
| LastDeplorables.com | Fake news | Scottsdale, Ariz. |
| LearnProgress.org | Some fake stories | Scottsdale, Ariz. |
| Liberty-Courier.com | Fake news | Orem, Utah |
| LiberalPlug.com | Fake news | Scottsdale, Ariz. |
| LibertyAlliance.com | Fake news | Dallas, Ga. |
| Local31News.com | Imposter site | Scottsdale, Ariz. |
| LondonWebNews.com | Some fake stories | Panama, Pa. |
| MacedoniaOnline.eu | Some fake stories | Macedonia |
| MadWorldNews.com | Fake news | Scottsdale, Ariz. |
| MajorThoughts.com | Fake news | Sunrise, Fla. |
| MediaMaxZone.com | Some fake stories | Trelawny, Jamaica |
| Mentor2day.com | Some fake stories | Scottsdale, Ariz. |
| MetropolitanWorlds.com | Fake news | Accra, Ghana |

| | | |
|---|---|---|
| MIssissippiHerald.com | Imposter site | Toronto, Canada |
| Nation.com.pk | Some fake stories | Lahore, Pakistan |
| NationalReport.net | Parody site | Scottsdale, Ariz. |
| NativeAmericans.us | Some fake stories | Cary, N.C. |
| NativeStuff.us | Fake news | Drenas, Kosovo |
| NBC.com.co | Imposter site | Phoenix, Ariz. |
| NeonNettle.com | Fake news | Toronto, Canada |
| Nephef.com | Fake news | Panama, Pa. |
| NewPoliticsToday.com | Fake news | Kumanovo, Macedonia |
| News4KTLA.com | Imposter site | Scottsdale, Ariz. |
| NewsBreakHere.com | Fake news | domain available |
| NewsForMeToday.com | Some fake stories | GoDaddy |
| NewsBreaksHere.com | Fake news | Chesterbrook, Pa. |
| NewsBreakingsPipe.com | Fake news | Limassol, Cyprus |
| NewsBySquad.com | Fake news | Panama, Pa. |

| | | |
|---|---|---|
| NewsConservative.com | Fake news | Panama, Pa. |
| NewsDaily12.com | Imposter site | Scottsdale, Ariz. |
| NewsExaminer.net | Fake news | Nobby Beach, Australia |
| NewsFeedHunter.com | Fake news | Panama, Pa. |
| NewsForMeToday.com | Fake news | GoDaddy |
| NewsLeak.co | Fake news | Tblisi, Georgia |
| Newslo.com | Parody site | Thessaloniki, Greece |
| NewsJustForYou1.blogspot.com | Fake news | Mountain View, Calif. |
| NewsOfTrump.com | Fake news | Panama, Pa. |
| NewsPhD.com | Fake news | GoDaddy |
| NewsUpToday.com | Fake news | GoDaddy |
| NewzMagazine.com | Fake news | Scottsdale, Ariz. |
| NNettle.com | Fake news | Toronto, Canada |
| NotAllowedTo.com | Fake news | https://www.whois.com/whois/notallowedto.com |
| Now8News.com | Imposter site | Scottsdale, Ariz. |

| | | |
|---|---|---|
| Nunadisbereel.com | Parody site | GoDaddy |
| NYDailyNews-TV.com | Imposter site | Wild West Domains |
| ObserverOnline.news | Imposter site | Panama, Pa. |
| OnePoliticalPlaza.com | Fake news | Miami, Fla. |
| OurLandoftheFree.com | Parody site | GoDaddy |
| OpenMagazines.com | Fake news | Scottsdale, Ariz. |
| PatriotCrier.com | Fake news | Scottsdale, Ariz. |
| PatriotUSA.website | Fake news | Panama, Pa. |
| Persecutes.com | Fake news | Scottsdale, Ariz. |
| PoliticalMayhem.news | Fake news | Scottsdale, Ariz. |
| Politicalo.com | Parody site | Jerusalem, Israel |
| Politicass.com | Parody site | Jerusalem, Israel |
| Politicono.com | Parody site | Jerusalem, Israel |
| Politicops.com | Parody site | Jerusalem, Israel |
| Politicot.com | Parody site | Jerusalem, Israel |
| PoliticsPaper.com | Fake news | GoDaddy |
| PoliticsUSANews.com | Fake news | Panama, Pa. |

| | | |
|---|---|---|
| PositiveDaily.com | Some fake stories | Kirkland, Wash. |
| Postcard.news | Some fake stories | Scottsdale, Ariz. |
| President45DonaldTrump.com | Fake news | Burlington, Mass. |
| Prntly.com | Fake news | Nobby Beach, Australia |
| ProudLeader.com | Fake news | North Waterboro, Me. |
| PuppetStringNews.com | Fake news | Jacksonville, FL |
| React365.com | Imposter site | GoDaddy |
| ReadConservatives.news | Fake news | Kirkland, Wash. |
| RealNewsRightNow.com | Parody site | Los Angeles, Calif. |
| RearFront.com | Fake news | Panama, Pa. |
| RedCountry.us | Fake news | Veles, Macedonia |
| RedInfo.us | Fake news | Veles, Macedonia |
| RedPolitics.us | Fake news | Veles, Macedonia |
| RedRockTribune.com | Imposter site | Scottsdale, Ariz. |
| ReflectionofMind.org | Some fake stories | Kirchhem Teck, Germany |
| Religionlo.com | Parody site | Jerusalem, Israel |

| Site | Type | Location |
|---|---|---|
| ReligionMind.com | Fake news | Balangoda, Sri Lanka |
| Revolutions2040.com | Fake news | GoDaddy |
| Rogue-Nation3.com | Fake news | Quebec, Canada |
| RumorJournal.com | Fake news | Panama, Pa. |
| SatiraTribune.com | Parody site | Scottsdale, Ariz. |
| Smag31.com | Some fake stories | Dundalk, Ireland |
| Snoopack.com | Fake news | Panama, Pa. |
| SocialEverythings.com | Fake news | Mahawela, Sri Lanka |
| SouthernConservativeExtra.com | Fake news | Came up as available for use |
| Spinzon.com | Fake news | Panama, Pa. |
| States-TV.com | Fake news | Scottsdale, Ariz. |
| StillnessInTheStorm.com | Some fake stories | Scottsdale, Ariz. |
| StGeorgeGazette.com | Fake news | Chesterbrooke, Pa |
| Success-Street.com | Fake news | Kumanovo, Macedonia |
| SupremePatriot.com | Fake news | Panama, Pa. |
| TDTAlliance.com | Fake news | Scottsdale, Ariz. |

| | | |
|---|---|---|
| TeaParty.org | Some fake stories | Laguna Woods, Calif. |
| TeddyStick.com | Some fake stories | Panama, Pa. |
| TEOinfo.com | Fake news | Kobenhavn, Denmark |
| ThatViralFeed.net | Some fake stories | Denver, Colo. |
| The-Insider.co | Fake news | Scottsdale, Ariz. |
| ThePremiumNews.com | Fake news | Panama, Pa. |
| The-Postillon.com | Parody site | Roubaix, France |
| TheBigRiddle.com | Some fake stories | Scottsdale, Ariz. |
| TheConservativeTreehouse.com | Some fake stories | Wild West Domains |
| TheExaminer.site | Fake news | Veles, Macedonia |
| TheGatewayPundit.com | Some fake stories | GoDaddy |
| The-Global-News.com | Fake news | Denver, CO |
| TheInternetPost.net | Fake news | Scottsdale, Ariz. |
| TheLastLineOfDefense.org | Parody site | Scottsdale, Ariz. |
| TheMiamiGazette.com | Imposter site | GoDaddy |

| | | |
|---|---|---|
| TheMoralOfTheStory.us | Fake news | Paradise, Calif. |
| TheNationalMarijuanaNews.com | Some fake stories | Henderson, Nev. |
| TheNet24h.com | Fake news | Brisbane, Australia |
| TheNewYorkEvening.com | Imposter site | Kumanovo, Macedonia |
| ThePoliticalInsider.com | Some fake stories | Scottsdale, Ariz. |
| TheRacketReport.com | Fake news | GoDaddy |
| TheRealShtick.com | Parody site | says domain available |
| TheRightists.com | Parody site | Jerusalem, Israel |
| TheRooster.com | Some fake stories | Scottsdale, Ariz. |
| ThePeoplesCube.com | Parody site | GoDaddy |
| TheSeattleTribune.com | Parody site | Scottsdale, Ariz. |
| TheSmokersClub.com | Some fake stories | Scottsdale, Ariz. |
| TheSolExchange.com | Some fake stories | Scottsdale, Ariz |
| TheTrumpMedia.com | Fake news | Scottsdale, Ariz. |
| TheUSA-News.com | Fake news | Chesterbrook, Pa. |

| | | |
|---|---|---|
| TheUSAConservative.com | Fake news | Scottsdale, Ariz. |
| TheWashingtonPress.com | Imposter site | Laurium, Mich. |
| TheWorldUpdate.com | Fake news | Scottsdale, Arz. |
| ThirdEstateNewsGroup.com | Fake news | Scottsdale, Arz. |
| Times.com.mx | Imposter site | Chesterbrook, Pa |
| TMZWorldNews.com | Fake news | Scottsdale, Ariz. |
| TopInfoPost.con | Some fake stories | Scottsdale, Ariz. |
| TrueAmericans.me | Fake news | Chesterbrook, Pa. |
| TrueTrumpers.com | Fake news | Chesterbrook, Pa. |
| UndergroundNewsReport.com | Fake news | Scottsdale, Ariz. |
| UniversePolitics.com | Fake news | Veles, Macedonia |
| UrbanImageMagazine.com | Some fake stories | Marion, Indiana |
| Urdoca.com | Some fake stories | Matale, Sri Lanka |
| USTruthWIre.com | Fake news | Panama, PA |
| USA360-TV.com | Fake news | Wild West Domains |

| | | |
|---|---|---|
| USA-Radio.com | Fake news | Scottsdale, Ariz. |
| USA-Television.com | Imposter site | Scottsdale, Ariz. |
| USADailyInfo.com | Fake news | Panama, PA |
| USADailyPost.us | Fake news | Veles, Macedonia |
| USADailyTime.com | Fake news | Panama, Pa. |
| USADoseNews.com | Fake news | Nobby Beach, Australia |
| USAFirstInformation.com | Fake news | Panama, Pa. |
| USANews4U.us | Fake news | Veles, Virgin Islands |
| USANewsToday.com | Fake news | Scotts, Mich. |
| USAPoliticsNow.com | Fake news | Nobby Beach, Australia |
| USAPolitics24hrs.com | Fake news | Nobby Beach, Australia |
| USAPoliticsToday.com | Fake news | Brea, Calif. |
| USAPoliticsZone.com | Fake news | Veles, Macedonia |
| USASnich.com | Fake news | Scottsdale, Ariz. |
| USATodayNews.me | Imposter site | Chesterbrook, Pa |
| USAWorldBox.com | Fake news | Panama, Pa. |

| | | |
|---|---|---|
| USHealthyAdvisor.com | Fake news | Panama, Pa. |
| USHealthyLife.com | Fake news | Panama, Pa. |
| USHerald.com | Fake news | Austin, Texas |
| USInfoNews.com | Fake news | Veles, Macedonia |
| USADailyThings24.com | Fake news | says domain available |
| USANewsflash.com | Fake news | Brea, CA |
| USANewsHome.com | Fake news | Scottsdale, Ariz. |
| USPoliticsInfo.com | Fake news | Toronto, Canada |
| USPOLN.com | Fake news | Scottsdale, Ariz. |
| USPostman.com | Fake news | Veles, Macedonia |
| USASupreme.com | Fake news | Scottsdale, Ariz. |
| USAConservativeReport.com | Fake news | GoDaddy |
| VeteransForDonaldTrump.com | Fake news | GoDaddy |
| ViralActions.com | Fake news | Scottsdale, Ariz. |
| VoxTribune.com | Fake news | Scottsdale, Ariz. |
| WashingtonEvening.com | Imposter site | Kumanovo, Macedonia |
| WashingtonFeed.com | Imposter site | Vancouver, Canada |

| | | |
|---|---|---|
| WashingtonPost.com.co | Imposter site | Washington, DC |
| WazaNews.tk | Fake news | Amsterdam, Netherlands |
| WeConservative.com | Fake news | Veles, Macedonia |
| WeekendPoliticalNews.com | Fake news | Panama, Pa. |
| WeLoveNative.com | Some fake stories | Pristina, Kosovo |
| WeTheProudPatriots.com | Fake news | Brea, CA |
| Werk35.com | Imposter site | says domain available |
| WestfieldPost.com | Imposter site | GoDaddy |
| WhatDoesItMean.com | Fake news | Yarmouth, CA |
| WhyDontYouTryThis.com | Some fake stories | GoDaddy |
| WorldNewsCircle.com | Fake news | Brea, CA |
| WorldNewsDailyReport.com | Parody site | Nobby Beach, Australia |
| WorldPoliticsNow.com | Fake news | Nassau, Bahamas |
| World.Politics.com | Fake news | Fort Lauderdale, FL |

| WorldTruth.tv | Fake news | GoDaddy |
| WRPM33.com | Imposter site | GoDaddy |
| WY21news.com | Imposter site | GoDaddy |
| YourNewsWire.com | Fake news | GoDaddy |

# CHAPTER 11 REPORTING FAKE NEWS ON THE WEB, SOCIAL MEDIA

As you will see below, not all entities comprising the World Wide Web currently has systems, tools, and countermeasures in place to address the spread of fake news. However, some of them are now working to put measures in place. Let's starts with the big names in social media.

FACEBOOK

Facing criticisms that it failed to deliver on its promise to help fight the spread of fake news in its platform three years after it initially announced its commitment, social media giant Facebook has finally taken action and has rolled out one feature in their post reporting tool: the False News button.

At the time of this writing, users can report a fake news by following these steps:

On the post, click the ... in the upper right corner.

Select the 'Give feedback on this video' option.

Select the 'False News' option.

Click the 'Send' button.

In its newsroom, Facebook Vice President for News Feed, Adam Mosseri, maintains a page that gets updated as the social media network continues to create mechanisms for the platform and for everyone to counter the spread of fake news.

In the release, Mosseri says that the countermeasures against fake news on the platform are focused on three areas:

Disruption of economic incentives as most fake news stories are motivated by financial profit,

Building new products to help stop the spread of fake news, and

Educating people in order for them to make informed decisions when they come across fake news stories.

By working with third party fact-checking organizations, Facebook has come up with various ways related to disrupting the monetary incentives of people who spread fake news:

Users will now see fewer ads and posts in News Feed that are linked to low-quality web pages.

Users will now be able to see consistency in video thumbnails and actual ad contents, as cloaking has been addressed.

Users will no longer see advertisements from advertisers who repeatedly share stories that are marked as false.

Facebook's partnership with third party fact-checkers means that it's working with organizations who are also signatories to Poynter's International Fact Checking Code of Principles. The findings in these partnerships, along with data collected from Facebook users themselves, allows for more validation and the consequent removal of fake content in platform. Here's an additional information related to the fact-checking work being done by Facebook.

In addition, Facebook also offers its users some tips in order to stop fake news and promptly report them:

Be critical of headlines. Fake news are represented by catchy headlines. These headlines are written in a way that words are manipulated in order to induce the desired response from readers. If headlines are outlandish and are too good to be true, they probably are.

Pay attention to the URL. Fake news websites are good at mimicry. From the URL down to the typography of their pages, they can effectively dupe readers into thinking that they have been redirected to the website's legitimate counterpart. But looking at the URL can save you that one click. For example, abcnews.com.co was used so that people will take it to be the official ABC News website. In reality, ABC's official news portal is abcnews.go.com.

Investigate the origin. The source of a story matters a lot. And because publication giants are easily recognized, readers won't have trouble verifying their content's legitimacy. But not all ethical publishers are popular. So readers must make it a point that when verifying a story, they should always inform themselves by learning more about the source of the story. A website's About page is one good way of verifying who the source of the story is.

Credible visual representation. While some fake news story outlets take time to design their websites and create copy complete with grammar check and all, some, if not most, do not exactly go that far. From experience, readers will know that a credible website has a professional look and has rare issues with typos and content presentation. In other words, the formatting has to be professionally done.

Be skeptical of imagery. Time and time again, Internet users have fallen prey to images that while authentic, have been used differently from its original context. Readers should observe caution by verifying the source of these photos. It is true that some photos (and videos) can elicit a strong emotional response especially if it is in line with the story. But with proper care, users can save themselves the emotional burden by checking the origin of the image first. Hint: you can use the Image Search function in Google.

Check the sources. In order to appear clever, fake news stories can cite sources. And while the people being quoted in these stories exist, the statements or actions attributed to them may not be true. What readers can do is to search for the name of that person and see what recent news is associated with him or her.

Again, check the source.

Verify the content. Not all fake news sites disguise themselves as legitimate organizations. Some websites actually make it a point of telling readers that they create satirical content or more directly, they create fake content.

Share what is credible. Think about your reputation as the 'sharer' of a story. If the people you know eventually find out that you have shared a fake story, what will they think of you? Some stories are intentionally fake. So you use your better judgment and do your own due diligence before sharing something.

TWITTER

Twitter has taken a more controversial stance on curbing the tons of fake news propagating in its own atmosphere. In February of this year, it's taken a criticism over its decision. In an article published by Callum Borchers of The Washington Post, he writes his reaction to Twitter's decision to keep its distance from fake news:

'There are lots of things you can't do on Twitter. You can't threaten violence, post pornography or wear a swastika in your profile pic. But you can lie. Twitter made clear on Thursday that while it is happy to serve as a platform for fact-checkers, it does not want to get into the business of making its own judgments about what is true or false.'

Nicole Lee, a writer at Engadget, responds in the same way:

"But leaving it up to the public to figure out what's real and what's fake isn't enough.

As much as Twitter doesn't want to be the "arbiter of truth," it should take some responsibility for safeguarding the community from falsehood and disinformation. If it isn't the arbiter of truth, it should at least try not to be the disseminator of lies."

It can be recalled that in mid-2017, Twitter announced that they're working on a button that allows users to report a tweet as fake. It was then followed by an announcement that they abandoned the project for fear that it would be gamed.

This is because days before the Washington Post reported on the fake news button prototype, President Trump tweeted: 'So they caught Fake News CNN cold, but what about NBC, CBS & ABC? What about the failing @nytimes & @washingtonpost? They are all Fake News!'

One can see the implication of that tweet. Sharing the same sentiment was Matthew Ingram, a previous reporter for Fortune, tweeting, 'I can almost guarantee that every CNN and NYT post that goes up will get flagged.'

So for now, Twitter users are left with the classic option of reporting fake news as not fake but as a spam (or maybe as something abusive or harmful). Here's what you can do:

Click the chevron icon

Choose the 'Report Tweet' option

Choose spam from the radio button options

Click 'Next'

Choose your preferred course of action

Click 'Done.'

You can choose to read more about Twitter's How to Report a Spam and How to Report Violations.

INSTAGRAM

For a social media platform that relies heavily on images, one would assume that users are responsible. That's true until fake news sent social media platforms reeling over ethics and disinformation. Unfortunately, Instagram, a platform acquired by Facebook, is not an exception.

Just recently, ABC News in Australia has published a report about teenagers who create fake Instagram accounts in order to destroy their peers' reputations. These impersonators were referred to as 'finstas.' In speaking with ANC News, Australia's eSafety Commissioner revealed that 40% of the complaints they get involve finstas. Note that not all finstas are used to illegal and bad activities.

Using the situation above, one can see that a double jeopardy is in place. One, there's impersonation. And two, there's fake news involved. So what things does Instagram have in place? Currently, it has policies involving Impersonation Accounts and Spam & Abuse.

For people who find out that someone has been impersonating them, all they need to do is to report the fake account alongside a government-issued photo ID. They have forms available for those who have an existing Instagram account and those who do not. People can refer to their Impersonation Accounts page for more details.

To report a spam or abuse, people can do two things: they can report a specific post or they can report an entire profile.

To report a post:

Tap on the three dots above the post

Tap 'Report'

Follow the onscreen instructions

To report a profile:

Tap on the three dots above the profile page

Tap 'Report'

Follow the onscreen instructions

For more information, people can refer to Instagram's Abuse & Spam page.


## LINKEDIN

Yes, a social media network devoted to professionals can also be a target for the propagation of fake news or information. And LinkedIn has a comprehensive set of instructions for people to follow when it comes to reporting Inappropriate Messages, Inappropriate Content, or Safety Concerns. Let's take a look at each of them.

Fake Profiles

Fake profiles can be pages that impersonate other people, empty profiles, profiles with fake names, or profiles that contain profanity. To report a fake profile:

Click the ... icon on the member's profile

Click the Report/Block icon

Select 'Report this profile' in the 'What do you want to do?' pop-up window.

Select the applicable reason for flagging the profile in the 'Tell us a little more' pop-up window.

Click 'Submit'

Inaccurate Profiles

Inaccurate profiles also fall within the realm of fake news. While 'inaccurate' is used, some people deliberately include details about their personal or professional background that are entirely fabricated.

To report an inaccurate profile, a formal complaint must be launched by using LinkedIn's 'Notice of Inaccurate Profile Information' form.

Hacked Accounts

Hacked accounts can be used as mediums to spread disinformation. As a consequence, the real person behind the profile may end up being totally discredited.

At times, one person may feel that one of his or her connection's account is hacked. For both, the process of reporting can be found in the Reporting a Hacked Account page.

Scams

Fake information used with the intention to scam people are also in place on LinkedIn.

There are four types of scams the social media platform recognizes:

Inheritance or advance fee fraud scams, which is characterized by LinkedIn as, 'scams [that] usually request a small fee up front in order to receive a large sum of money in return.

Job scams characterized as involving 'people pretending to be recruiters or employers offering high-paying jobs for little work. These can include mystery shopper, work from home or personal assistant scams.'

Technical support scams as offers for help from within LinkedIn with a corresponding fee.

Dating and romance scams coming from people who contact other people expressing interest in a romantic relationship. For this one, it should be noted that LinkedIn was established as a professional platform and not as a dating site.

To report any of these types of scams, you can follow the instructions on the Recognizing and Reporting Scams page.

LinkedIn also has a dedicated reporting feature its acquisition, SlideShare which can be found on the Flagging Inappropriate Content on SlideShare.

YOUTUBE

Google's video-sharing platform application, YouTube, could be a little late in joining the fight-fake-news bandwagon. Nonetheless, it announced specific plans in early 2018 on how to combat the proliferation of fake content within its platform, among others. But right now, the process in place to report a video with fake content is as follows:

Click the ... on the lower right corner of a video.

Choose 'Report.'

Tick the applicable radio button.

Choose from the dropdown fields.

Click 'Next.'

Follow the onscreen prompts.


SNAPCHAT

Snapchat can pride itself as a social media platform that has never been embroiled in the proliferation of fake news. A report from five fact-checking organizations around the world say that it has never seen a fake news on the platform. But wanting to get ahead of the game, and wanting to distance itself from the problems currently challenging the likes of Facebook, Twitter, and YouTube, Snapchat has rolled out an update that includes a redesign of the app's interface.

While the redesign has received backlash, Evan Spiegel, co-founder and CEO, said that the redesign was meant to further insulate it from the threat of fake news polluting its platform. The mechanism? Human editors get to curate content and pick the ones that can be promoted. Unlike Snapchat, giants Facebook and Twitter currently follows a reactive approach by using an algorithm to flag cases of fake news, to block profiles, and to ban advertisers.

But apart from the latest update, Katie Sanders, deputy editor of Politifact, points out that one reason Snapchat may be well-insulated from fake news is that users use the app for an entirely different purpose.

She says, "I don't think it's regarded as a news source. You wouldn't go to Snapchat necessarily to get the latest on the Las Vegas shooting. I think people probably use Snapchat differently."

On top of that, there is really no mechanism for a snap to go viral on the app. Still, processes are in place within Snapchat for users to report cases of abuse and stories on the web.

## WHATSAPP

WhatsApp is a service owned by Facebook but despite its owner struggling to combat the proliferation of fake news within its platform, WhatsApp seems to be preparing its own countermeasure.

This countermeasure involves shared links or messages that have been forwarded more than 25 times. If that happens, an in-app notification appears when a user is about to forward the same message.

Now, in some cases, users will need to send a single message to multiple users. To accommodate this function without triggering a warning, WhatsApp encourages users to use the Broadcast List feature.

But that's not the only way WhatsApp has devised a countermeasure to fight fake news. In Egypt, WhatsApp launched a hotline for people to 'report news that aims to "to endanger the nation's security or public interests.'

Egypt's citizens can report any of the fabricated news violations by sending messages to the General Prosecution office via the Whatsapp hotline.

In Malaysia, the Malaysian Communications and Multimedia Commission or MCMC has set up a portal called sebenarnya.my. This portal is created for the purpose of curbing the spread of fake news and was triggered by a viral message circulated to WhatsApp users in the country. The message goes: 'From another (chat) group. But don't know whether it's true or not.'

## TUMBLR

In a news report published by The Guardian in March 2018, it revealed that Tumblr has uncovered 84 accounts linked to 13 people who are affiliated with a Russia's Internet Research Agency. The IRA is a troll farm and was known to have an influence over the US 2016 presidential elections.

In response, Tumblr said that it will be sending an emailing anyone who followed an IRA-linked account, who liked, who replied to, or who reblogged any posts linked to the IRA. However, it said that users will still have an option on whether or not to delete the content from their account. The email will only serve to inform.

Tumblr also mentioned that apart from the email, it will also be maintaining a record of all IRA-linked usernames on a publicly accessible database.

Finally, the report also quotes Tumblr saying that it [Tumblr] 'is committed to terminating accounts in the future if it finds them to be affiliated with "disinformation campaigns," and alerting law enforcement of their identities. "Be aware that people want to manipulate the conversation," the post reads. "Knowing that disinformation and propaganda accounts are out there makes it harder for them to operate.'

## GOOGLE

Among all others mentioned in this chapter, perhaps Google is experiencing the most pressure when it comes to its efforts in combatting fake news.

Apart from Google Forums getting inundated with questions such as, 'How do I report a fake news on a search result?,' Campaign for Accountability has published a damning report that despite the knowledge of fake news circulating within the search engine, Google still displays ads of the same nature within its advertising network.

The report, called the Google Transparency Project, revealed that right-wing content publishers, which are often responsible for spreading misleading information, are responsible for Google's $48.8 million annual revenue. On top of that, the Google Display Network, which is a group of about two million pre-approved websites, has contributed to the company's first quarter revenue in 2017 amounting to $4 billion. In response, Google was reported to be taking action in three ways.

First, in a story published by Engadget, Google is taking steps in order to revamp its snippet feature. These snippets are the short descriptions people see on the list of search results in support of a headline.

Undoubtedly, the snippets area can be used in order to highlight information which may be fake. The story continues to detail that Google can lend more quality to these snippets by improving the company's Search Quality Rater Guidelines. In turn, the guideline will help human raters flag conspiracy theories, false information, offensive information, and hoaxes more accurately.

Second, Google also said that it will introduce measures in order to promote high-quality content and relegate those with low-quality content to lower position in the search results.

Third, users may begin to see more than one snippet as they browse through the search results list top pick a page they want to view. As an addition, users will have the power to report snippets that they suspect to be fake. A link will be found below the snippets in question themselves.

Now, in February, Quartz Media published a story about how Google executives has been floating another idea to combat fake news to its fellow attendees. The idea borders around predictive prompts where notifications will prompt users 'whether information is trustworthy before they shared it on social networks like Facebook and Twitter.'

And in March, Reuters released a report saying that Google 'is launching the Google News Initiative, to weed out fake news online and during breaking news situations.' The report further states that for the next three years, Google plans to spend $300 million over the next three years 'to improve the accuracy and quality of news appearing on its platforms.' Alongside that, Google will also be launching a tool that will allow users to subscribe to reputable news publications.

So while Google is yet to issue a definite mechanism to combat the spread of fake news within its networks, it seems that they are working on building mechanisms as a countermeasure.

In the next two and final chapters of this eBook, we will look at specific countermeasures in different countries – where there are indications that something is being done through legislation, and what end user can do be more vigilant and help curb the spread of fake news.

# CHAPTER 12 FAKE NEWS COUNTERMEASURES: COUNTRIES

The reach of fake news and its adverse effects is not only felt in the United States. Recently, a string of legislation has been going around in some countries around the world. Let's take a look at how the international community has set up countermeasures against fake news.

GERMANY

The country might hold the dubious title of being the first nation to introduce laws that criminalizes fake news.

Through the Net Enforcement Act, the country aims to criminalize the publication of unlawful content, including issuing false statements and untrue assertions that may seriously affect the country's external security and diplomatic relationships.

The law also covers defamation, incitement of hatred, making threats, and dissemination of pornography and pornographic materials.

In relation to social media, the Net Enforcement Act requires platforms like Twitter, Facebook, and YouTube are required to block or to remove unlawful content from their portals within seven days for all content found to be unlawful or within 24 hours upon submission of complaint.

As for the offenses, a fine of up to 500,000 or 5 million euros will be imposed.

The law was enacted on 01 January 2018. However, recent reports began to circulate about how a new coalition of politicians is planning to amend it by introducing a provision that makes it possible for users to request for blocked or delete content to be unblocked or re-published if done by mistake.

The Net Enforcement Act was established ahead of the September 2017 elections.

## FRANCE

Another European country is eyeing to establish a new law in order to combat fake news on social media and websites. The planned law will also require websites to be transparent by revealing how much money was spent on advertisements. In addition to that, websites will also be required to impose a cap on the amount of money that may be used in advertisements.

The proposal was announced by now President Emmanuel Macron – a victim of fake news during his campaign for presidency.

As of this writing, the planned law is not yet tabled.

## THE PHILIPPINES

As of this writing, three bills are pending on the country's congressional and senate chambers.

First, Senate Bill No. 1942 was proposed in order to criminalize the distribution of fake news. The bill defined fake news as having the following elements:

Malicious intent

Published online, on broadcast, or in print

Causes violence, chaos, hate, panic, or propaganda that discredits a person's reputation

The source knows that the information is false

The penalties proposed are a fine of $95,000 with a maximum of five years in jail for the primary offender and $57,000 with a maximum of three years in jail for the accomplice.

The proposed bill also specifies that any public official guilty of such offense will be subject to double the amount in fines and will be perpetually disqualified from public office.

As for social media platforms that fail to remove fake news content within a reasonable period following the knowledge of such falsity will be fined $383,000 and will face time between 10 to 20 years in jail.

Second, House Bill No. 6022 is a bill that prohibits the creation and distribution of fake news. The bill defines 'fake news' as something that is fabricated, presented in an edited audio or video format in a manner that distorts facts, and leads to the distortion, misquotation, or inaccurate report of a person's statement.

The proposed penalties under this bill is cumulative, with mass media outlets risking to be fined $19,000 for creating fake news stories and $9,000 for spreading fake content the first instance.

Social media users who are found guilty will face a first-time penalty that includes a $1,000 fine for creating fake news stories and a $900 fine for its distribution. On top that, offenders will also face potential jail time.

Finally, Senate Bill No. 1680 is a proposal directed to people who work in public service and those who work for them. The bill seeks to criminalize dissemination of false information to the public.

In response to the three pending bills, President Rodrigo Duterte said that none of them may be approved by the Congress reiterating that lawmakers should focus on the amending the punishment for defamation instead.

SINGAPORE

Another Asian country to take fake news seriously is Singapore. With its citizens supporting the move to create more stringent laws when it comes to the correction or removal of fake news.

Prior to the Law and Affairs Home Minister's announcement, a poll was conducted showing that three in four people could tell at the very first instance that a news story is fake.

As of this writing, an 8-day public hearing that involves the parliament has just concluded and whether or not a new law should be enacted is still pending.

During the duration of the hearing, Facebook and Twitter has been reported to provide their sentiments over the country's prospective move. Facebook pointed out that the country already has existing laws to tackle fake news, hate speech, and defamation.

Twitter, on the other hand, said that no institution should decide on whether or not something is true.

INDONESIA

On 03 January 2018, the country has created a cyber-security agency to strengthen its efforts in dealing with fake news, hate speech, religious extremism, and terrorism.

MALAYSIA

In March 2018, the Anti-Fake News 2018 bill was introduced to the Malaysian parliament. The bill seeks to impose up to 10 years of prison time for anyone who knowingly creates, distributes, or publishes fake news with a fine of $26,000.

The term 'fake news' is defined in the bill as something that includes 'news, information, data and reports that are wholly or partly false.' The bill also includes a clause saying that it applies to organization or individuals who, despite being out of the country, creating fake news that involves the country or its citizens.

In the final chapter, let us focus on the point of view of the end user – you – on what you can in terms of due diligence involving possible fake news.

# CHAPTER 13   DUE DILIGENCE TO SPOT FAKE NEWS

Ultimately, the initial gatekeepers of fake news are the end users. Every day, billions of Internet users prowl the World Wide Web in search for information and to share information for different purposes. While countries and online organizations, companies, and other entities are working to place countermeasure mechanisms to combat the proliferation of fake news, it is the end user's responsibility to exercise proper judgment before sharing a specific piece of content. The challenge here is that not everyone is able to exercise better judgment on the pieces of information they come across with online. It may not always be about laziness; it is the lack of knowledge that may be attributed to the unintentional spreads of fake news. So in this final chapter, let's take a look at some of the ways that each of us can become responsible ambassadors of online content.

LOOKING FOR THE SIGNS OF FAKE NEWS

Fake news are often cloaked with beautiful and striking headlines. They might be accompanied by powerful images, and they may be supported by subheading that evoke strong emotional reactions. In effect, these emotional reactions become the triggers to an information being shared. But before your judgment gets clouded by how you feel, you might want to pause for a bit and consider what you think. Start from what you see.

Is the headline hyperbolic?

Merriam-Webster defines hyperbole succinctly as an extravagant exaggeration [of something.] Hyperbolic headlines are also referred to as clickbait headlines. These are headlines that serve one purpose: to cause readers to do one thing: to click on the link and be directed to a web page. So if you come across a headline that is outlandish, chances are, its fake content.

Is the domain strange?

Granted that you have taken the bait and made that click, take notice of the domain. Often, fake news websites imitate legitimate websites. This is especially true for news outlets. If you are not sure, open a new tab and put in a search for the domain name.

Is the website layout weird?

Legitimate websites always make it a point to structure their website in an organized and in a professional manner. No neon side bars, no glowing pop-ups, and no oversized texts. This is because legitimate websites are protective of their brand. With their website as their official representation before the world, they will not risk investing in cheap design and disorganized layout.

Does the content contain typographical and grammatical errors?

You do not have to be a grammar expert or someone who have a keen eye for detail so that you can spot nitty-gritty details on a web page. Play it by the eye. You can easily spot a typographical error as you read each word. And when you do read, also check how the sentences flow. Do they make sense or do they look spun and were never edited or proofed? Are they overflowing with excessive punctuations?

The importance of ensuring that content is well-structured and well-written goes back to the brand. A legitimate company does not want to lose its visitors over simple issues such as misusing 'its' for 'it's,' for example.

Do images or videos reflect quality?

Nowadays, images and videos can be edited to achieve the message intended by its creators. Therefore, they invest in professional editors who, in turn, use professional tools in order to achieve the level of quality that their clients expect. If you find that an image or a video is edited poorly, but are supposed to represent a reputable brand, you are right to question the website's credibility.

On another note, images used on websites must be traceable to their original versions. Often, you can trace where an image is taken from by clicking on it. In doing so, you should be directed to a page where it is taken and be presented with the unedited form. This is often time-consuming as you may end up bouncing from page to another, so the easier way would be for you to see if the author cited the image's source.

Now, you also have to be careful because there are image banks out there that do not require users to credit the person or institution who captured the image. So as a workaround, you can perform a Google Image search. Save the image to your computer and go to images.google.com. There, you will be prompted to upload the same image and see where it came from. From the results, you will also be able to see who used the same image on their web pages.

Does the content have a publication history?

Most applicable to news-related content and news-related websites, the publication history informs the reader how current a piece of writing is. Have you noticed that on some websites that you visit, there are notes saying something like, 'This post has been updated to...' or 'This post was last updated on...'? This signifies that the owner of the website is keeping abreast of the current information on topics that depend on time for proper context.

However, you should also distinguish between time-based and evergreen content. Evergreen content are types of content whose concepts do not change with time. For example – even though it is still being reputed – a blog post that asserts that the Earth is round need not have a date. It's a known fact and unless science itself disproves it, will stand to be true. The bottom line is for you to check whether the content you are looking it as outdated or if it is current.

Does it have reputable citations?

Citations, in the context of this discussion, includes information about the author of the article, data source annotations, and bibliography, if applicable. Now, anyone can cite anyone as a source. What you need to check here is the quality of the cited source. A debatable topic here is quoting Wikipedia as a source. With Wikipedia's open edit policy, it is inevitable that multiple sources for a single claim can change over time and that editors will have different ways of stating a single idea.

When you evaluate the reliability of a source, look for indications of credibility and authority. Is the person cited someone who is known in his or her industry? Does he or she hold a respectable position? For a cited work, was it published in a reputable platform? Is it being quoted by multiple people? Does it rank high in search results?

Does the content read like it's a satire?

If it does, then you have to be critical about it. Check the website's about section to know who they are and what they do. Some fake news websites mean well. They just approach their 'reporting' or 'content standards' differently by publishing satirical content. If a website claims beforehand that the information it provides is fake work, well and good. Be wary of websites that do not make the nature of their work clear. If you have other sources that are more reputable, use those instead.

Does the content read like a fact or an opinion?

Opinions are statement of beliefs so they are subjective. Meaning, they reflect the writer's point of view. In contrast, facts are objective and are verifiable. In other words, there's data or evidence to prove that a fact is a fact. When you come across a piece of information, you should be able distinguish between the two.

For opinions, expect that you won't always have to agree with the writer. But be careful; just because the opinion reflected in the article is inconsistent with your beliefs does not mean that it is fake. It is just a matter of the writer and you not sharing the same sentiments.

For facts, be sure that you have ways to verify the information that make up its factuality. Cross reference it online if you have to.

Who wrote the article?

Because they write fake content, there's a high chance that author names are fabricated. Legitimate writers, bloggers, or content creators maintain a public profile of themselves. Why? It is because they want to boot their authority out there. They want to maintain or to build their credibility. Some authors even have their own websites and their own professional brand pages on social media.

While a clever fake news writer may establish all of these, the collection of content he or she writes will be marked by consistent indications of falsehood. Evaluate their portfolio of work in the same way as you evaluate a piece of information suspected to be a fake.

But you know what? Some fake news writers actually are known and have built quite a reputation in the industry. If you spot one of their works, you are better off looking at another website.

Are you biased?

In Chapter 5, you saw a list of the different cognitive biases that may affect your judgment on whether or not a story is fake. Be careful of letting your biases influence your perception as you might end up sharing a story that is proven to be fake. Again, just because a certain piece of information fits right into your belief system means that it is true, and vice versa.

In sum, you need to be more responsible when sharing what you see online. If you feel that something needs verification, do your own diligence. The reach of something shared in social media cannot be predicted. Even for posts that promoted and ads that are boosted, reach figures are only cited as estimates. The key to effectively combatting the spread of fake news is media literacy. And while media regulation against fake news is beginning to take shape, it is still in its infancy and it is still highly debatable. So it all starts with you. Being a responsible individual, you should know that whatever you put out there may be seen by the public. And if you put something questionable out there, those people who believe in you will take it to be reliable. Extra care in information dissemination is warranted.

# CHAPTER 14 FINAL WORDS

Thank you for reading this book!

I hope that this book has created some alerts for fake news on you. And I hope that you can continue spreading the dangers of fake news and make our world more conscious and safer.

Be aware that hackers will improve their skills on creating and spreading fake news with better sites, content, forged sources, artificial intelligence, microtargeting and social media bots.

I also hope that you have become a citizen that demands a safer internet if you weren't already.

If you enjoyed this book, please take the time to share your thoughts and post a review on Amazon. It'd be greatly appreciated!

If you feel like there is room for improvement on this book, let me know how I can help you.

Thank you and good luck!

Fernando Uilherme Barbosa de Azevedo

www.ingramcontent.com/pod-product-compliance
Lightning Source LLC
Chambersburg PA
CBHW031429210526
45464CB00005B/2117